TRADE

MARK

One
Reel a
Week

The authors, Fred J. Balshofer and Arthur C. Miller, in front of a location in Calabasas, California, where Balshofer shot many pictures in the early days. This photograph was made in 1966.

One Reel a Week

by
FRED J. BALSHOFER
and
ARTHUR C. MILLER

with the assistance of
BEBE BERGSTEN

foreword by
KEMP R. NIVER

UNIVERSITY OF CALIFORNIA PRESS   BERKELEY & LOS ANGELES   1967

University of California Press
Berkeley and Los Angeles   1967

Cambridge University Press
London, England

The passage from Kenneth Macgowan's *Behind the Screen* is quoted by permission of Delacorte Press.

Contents

EARLY CAREER WITH SHIELDS, LUBIN AND OTHERS   1
(Balshofer)

THE EARLY FILM COMPANIES—CRESCENT AND BISON   14
(Balshofer)

MAKING *THE TRUE HEART OF AN INDIAN*   30
(Miller)

PATENTS COMPANY TROUBLES AND THE   38
DECISION TO MOVE WEST
(Balshofer)

WORKING FOR EDWIN S. PORTER   43
(Miller)

FILMING IN THE WILD WEST   54
(Balshofer)

WITH THE PATHÉ NEWS WEEKLY   68
(Miller)

THE KEYSTONE FILM COMPANY AND RIVALRY   74
AMONG THE COMPANIES
(Balshofer)

THE PERILS OF PAULINE   94
(Miller)

THE STERLING FILM COMPANY AND ACTOR   108
TROUBLES
   (Balshofer)

WORKING FOR GEORGE FITZMAURICE   122
   (Miller)

THE YORKE FILM CORPORATION   136
   (Balshofer)

FILMING MAE MURRAY, ELSIE FERGUSON,   143
RICHARD BARTHELMESS, AND OTHERS
   (Miller)

FILMING IN LONDON AND ROME   161
   (Miller)

WITH CECIL B. DeMILLE AND JOHN FORD   177
   (Miller)

LAST FILMS BEFORE RETIREMENT   189
   (Miller)

PICTORIAL APPENDIX   203

INDEX   211

Preface

ONCE IN A WHILE people interested in the history of motion pictures drop by the American Society of Cinematographers to study our collection of cameras and projectors which date from the pioneer days of the business. Invariably the conversation leads to the question, "How did you get started in the movies as a cameraman?" No short explanation ever satisfies the questioners, for the longer the conversation continues, the longer the inquiry continues. Curiosity grows as we discuss the early days of moviemaking, and inevitably our talks conclude with a remark such as, "You should write a book."

I gave no serious thought to this suggestion until one day I was reminiscing with an old friend, Fred Balshofer, who surprised me with a similar suggestion. "Arthur," he said, "you should write a book telling about those early days." The man with whom I had been talking is one of the pioneers of motion pictures and, in fact, the man from whom I learned my trade as a cameraman some fifty-seven years ago. Coming from him, somehow the idea sounded different. It demanded consideration. Well aware that being a cameraman did not qualify me as a writer, I tried to forget the whole idea but I just couldn't.

I thought it over for several days and came to the conclusion that together we might try to write an account of those fascinating early years, based mainly on the colorful career of Balshofer, who started in the moving picture business with the Lubin Company in Philadelphia in 1905. When I approached Fred with the idea, his first reaction was not encouraging. He, too, was reluctant to assume that writing was in his line. Our session prompted further talks every time we saw each other. Finally we decided to do it.

Numerous books have been published describing the history of the movies, usually consisting of page after page of photographs to illustrate the progress of the industry by introducing new stars to distinguish particular periods. Many biographies have been written about various screen personalities, all of which have been taken as gospel simply because the stories have been repeated so often they have been transformed into legends. As a result many statements in this history will appear to be contradictory. We have no axe to grind. We merely want to tell of the early days of moviemaking as we saw and lived them. Since this is a joint autobiography, each chapter is labeled with the teller's name.

A.M.

Foreword

by KEMP R. NIVER

T he pages of this book provide never before published
insights into many phases of the movie-making industry
in its exciting, formative years. The authors are uniquely
equipped to write such a book. Their lives span the period from
the very beginning of motion picture making in the United
States on into the 1950s, and their remarkable experiences are
presented in a forthright manner, without embellishment.

Fred Balshofer, a stereoscopic slide photographer, made the
transition from still photography to motion pictures when he
joined the Lubin Manufacturing Company in Philadelphia in
1905. After three colorful years of varied experiences with Lubin, Balshofer felt confident enough to launch a career as a producer, even though well aware that he faced being sued by "the
trust," or Motion Picture Patents Company, for doing so. In 1908
Balshofer founded the Crescent Film Company in Brooklyn
where he met and hired a local lad, Arthur Miller, then barely
fourteen years old, to help him develop film he photographed
during the day. Balshofer trained Miller to do laboratory work
and to crank a moving picture camera. Finding Miller an eager
pupil, Balshofer also taught him to expose film properly and
introduced him to photographic composition. So well did Balshofer teach Miller and so great was Miller's interest in the new
art that he became a master in the field. In the years that followed, Miller won three Oscars for motion picture photography,
was nominated seven times for the Academy Award, and the
results of his camera work received world-wide acclaim.

The financial returns from Crescent Film Company were such
that Balshofer began to realize the potentialities of this new and
fascinating type of entertainment. Fred Balshofer persuaded
Adam Kessel, a former bookmaker, and Charles O. Bauman,
once a streetcar conductor, to join him in founding what became
one of the largest of the independent movie producers, the New
York Motion Picture Company, with Bison and Keystone among
its subsidiaries. Balshofer's picturesque description of Holly-

wood as he found it when he brought his Bison company west in 1909, and the trials and tribulations he endured while eluding the Patents Company detectives, make fascinating reading.

Arthur Miller, considered too young to accompany Balshofer west, remained in New York to work for another motion picture pioneer, Edwin S. Porter of *The Great Train Robbery* fame; he eventually reached Hollywood in 1922, and for the next thirty years worked with nearly every important producer, director, and actor in the business. Ill health forced his retirement in the 1950s. Nevertheless, Miller still gets calls from directors of the stature of John Ford, with whom he made *How Green Was My Valley*, with requests such as, "Artie, come on, let's make another picture."

The chapters of *One Reel a Week*, written alternately by Balshofer and Miller, contain much movie history, and interestingly enough, chronicle the development of movie-making machinery as well.

Chapter 1

EARLY CAREER WITH SHIELDS, LUBIN, AND OTHERS

B EFORE I STARTED my career in the moving picture industry with the Lubin Manufacturing Company of Philadelphia in 1905, I had already had some experience. Most young people served an apprenticeship in those days and I was no exception. I was an apprentice with the firm of Stromeyer and Wyman in New York City, manufacturers of stereoscopic photographs. When they thought I was ready, they sent me out to make stereoscopic still pictures to supply the ever-growing demand for the twin-lensed handheld viewers that could be found on the parlor table in most homes. Looking at scenes of Niagara Falls, or Pike's Peak or Yellowstone Park in the third dimension was home entertainment in those days.

When I had been with Stromeyer and Wyman for about two years they moved to their new building in Arlington, New Jersey, a long trip for me. Not long after they moved, Stromeyer and Wyman sold out to Underwood and Underwood. I stayed with Underwood and was promoted to assistant manager. By this time the trip from my home in New York to Arlington had become exhausting, so I moved close to the plant, where I found a room in a boarding house operated by two old-maid sisters.

Some evenings I would visit the penny arcade in Newark, New Jersey, and, like other customers, I would drop a penny in the slot, then turn the crank that made one picture follow the previous one rapidly enough to create the effect of moving pictures. At that time there were two types of viewing machines.

One was the Edison Kinetoscope with a continuous strip of film. The other, manufactured by the American Mutoscope & Biograph Company, was called the Mutoscope and utilized paper prints. As one picture fell away, another was exposed, thus achieving the effect of a motion picture.

The subjects were varied and ranged from soldiers drilling, or a girl dancing, to a few rounds of a prize fight. Each picture lasted approximately one minute. Peep shows were a novelty but that is all that can be said for them.

As a photographer, naturally I was intrigued by the mechanical aspect, but my current job with Underwood and Underwood offered more of a challenge. Choosing subjects and compositions for the most suitable stereoscopic pictures was absorbing work, and, besides, my salary now was such that I had no reason to want to leave for this new field known as moving pictures.

After it became practical to project pictures on a screen, motion pictures were accorded recognition as an important industry. Several places on Fourteenth Street in New York showed short subjects such as *The Fireman's Parade on Fifth Avenue, Feeding the Pigeons in Central Park,* and the like.

In the fall of 1903 while I was on a holiday at Coney Island I saw the now-famous motion picture, *The Great Train Robbery,* directed and produced by Edwin S. Porter who was at that time working for the Thomas A. Edison Company. This moving picture told a story in a dramatic and suspenseful way, and it gave me the impression that I was seeing a stage play. As I thought about it on the trolley on my way home, I became more and more convinced that moving pictures were no longer a novelty but a growing entertainment business.

I soon found out that I was not the only one who had arrived at this conclusion. Exciting stories of the dime novel type were being shown in every possible place that could be rigged up for the purpose. In a little over a year, movie theaters, called nickelodeons because of their five-cent admission charge, were springing up in every large city. Nickelodeon theaters actually

were stores, with seats placed across from one side wall to the
other, and with an aisle down the center. At the rear of the
store was a screen for showing pictures, and to one side was
the piano player who changed his tune to suit the mood of the
current scene. At the front end, between the entrance and exit,
was a platform with a projection machine, high above the
heads of the audience. Fireproof booths were not a require-
ment although the film was highly inflammable. After several
fires, asbestos booths that enclosed the projecting machine and
the operator on the platform were marketed. These booths gave
the audience some feeling of safety. The exterior front of the
store was arranged with a ticket-selling booth in the center, an
entrance on one side, and the exit on the other.

About this time I was offered a job by the Shields Lantern
Slide Company in New York City. Shields offered me a nice
increase in salary, but what made the job even more enticing
was the location, which would make it possible for me to live
at home with my parents. I decided to take it.

As I look back, I think that leaving Underwood and Underwood after being with them for about eight years was the
hardest decision I ever had to make in my life. My new job,
however, turned out to be fascinating. I posed the players and
photographed illustrated slides for such popular songs of the
day as, "She Might Have Seen Better Days," "Just Tell Them
That You Saw Me," and "The Baggage Coach Ahead." I even
operated the stereoptican magic lantern for Gus Edwards when
he played in and around New York. From his later vaudeville
acts, "School Days," came such personalities as Eddie Cantor,
George Jessel, Walter Winchell, Groucho Marx, and many
others.

By the end of 1904, motion pictures had become so popular
that the slide business began to taper off. I timidly suggested
to Shields the possibility of making moving pictures as well as
lantern slides. Shields was a stubborn, pompous man and in his
typical, sarcastic manner, said, "Make moving pictures? Why
those flickering things hurt your eyes. They're just a passing
fancy." He was annoyed at my temerity and managed to make
my suggestion sound outright ridiculous.

I was well aware that he was not alone in his opinion. There were plenty of others who thought moving pictures were simply a fad. Consequently, Mr. Shields's negative response temporarily dampened my enthusiasm. I couldn't decide if my observation of the growing success of moving pictures was in error or whether my desire to find a place in this virgin field of photography caused me to make such a rash suggestion.

After two years with the Shields Lantern Slide Company, I had saved a little money, so I decided to take a vacation in south Jersey near Atlantic City. On the way home it was necessary to change trains in Philadelphia. I took the opportunity to take a few days to see the city. As I strolled along Eighth Street, my attention was caught by a store with the entrance between two plate glass windows. Gold letters on one window read "Siegmund Lubin, Optician" and on the other "Manufacturer of Moving Pictures." Moving pictures were now magic words to me, and on an impulse I entered the store. I hardly anticipated that this moment would change my career and start me in an industry where I would remain the rest of my working life.

After a moment Mr. Lubin came from the back of the store. He was a bald-headed, stoop-shouldered man, well over six feet tall, and when he talked he really mangled the English language. I told him I would like a job in his moving picture company. Lubin didn't say a word but looked me over like he was appraising a horse before buying it. I stood awkwardly embarrassed until he finally spoke. "You can vaste tousands of dollars if you don't know vat you are doing in diss moving picture business," was Lubin's first remark. "What makes you think I don't know what I'm doing?" I responded. "I know photography and I have been making illustrated song slides for the past two years." Mr. Lubin's sole reaction was a slight smile. Then I told him of my years with Underwood and Underwood. "You make money?" Lubin inquired. I told him I'd been doing just fine. "Then vy don't you stay in the singing business?"

I explained to Lubin that there had been a decline in the use of song slides and that I thought that moving pictures were a growing business. This seemed to make an impression on him and, after further conversation, we settled on a week's trial. I was so afraid I might not have a chance, even for a week, of learning something about the moving picture business that I forebore to ask Mr. Lubin how much he planned to pay me.

The real surprise was that for several weeks I never had the chance to photograph anything. I was kept busy in the laboratory in the basement of the store making duplicates of pictures that had been produced in France, by the Méliès company and Pathé Freres. We called them "dupes" from of course "duplicates." I simply printed a negative from a positive print and from that duped negative made as many positive prints as Lubin could sell to his customers. In those days each moving picture company had its own trademark which was usually placed in some prominent place in the picture to ensure its visibility. The Méliès trademark was a star, and Pathé used a rooster in a circle. I spent a lot of time blocking out the trademark on each individual frame under a magnifying glass, using a camel's hair brush dipped in opaque.

When customers came to the store to buy moving pictures, Mr. Lubin brought them down to the laboratory and I would show some of our duped pictures on a small screen. When the selection had been made, the customer paid in advance. Then I would make the prints to be shipped. It required little intelligence to know that this was shady business, but Mr. Lubin carried on the practice as if it were perfectly ordinary and completely legitimate.

At the end of the first week, Lubin came down to the laboratory and pressed a bill that had been folded to the size of a postage stamp into the palm of my hand. He squeezed my fingers around it and said, "You're my man." After he left, I unfolded the bill and found it was five dollars. This was almost nothing compared with what I had been earning. Nevertheless, I made up my mind that until I had had a chance to use a moving picture camera I was going to stay with Mr. Lubin. Each week the same placing of the folded bill in my hand continued, only the bills became larger in denomination. For some time, I believed this was a secret between us, but then I found out that Lubin went through the same routine with Jack Frawley, whom he called his general manager and director, and the other two young men who worked there. This manner of paying salaries was simply an idiosyncrasy of this pioneer film-maker who became known affectionately as "Pop" Lubin to others in the business.

Siegmund Lubin was about fifty-five then. He had come to America from his native Germany when he was eighteen and had learned the optical business in this country. In 1896 Lubin perfected a moving picture camera and began making movies. He started with a small laboratory in the cellar of his optical store, the same one where I worked. He had no studio so all his pictures were made outdoors, usually in Fairmont Park, a large and beautiful public park not far from the city.

Early in 1905, a few months after I joined him, he built a larger laboratory and a small studio in an old three-story building on Arch Street, directly opposite Brandenburg's Dime Museum, where movies and illustrated slides were shown. His Arch Street laboratory was on the top floor, with a small studio on the roof above it. The studio resembled those used for portraits except that it was larger. It had a conventional slanting roof of glass that gave us the only source of light for photography. Consequently, the small interiors had to be photographed during the sunny hours of the day which were rare in the stormy winter months. Interiors were avoided as much as possible. In the summer of 1907, Lubin went all out and established a new and modern studio equipped with Cooper-Hewitt lighting in a large, new building on Market Street in the heart of Philadelphia.

When I joined Lubin in 1905, other companies producing moving pictures were Méliès, Gaumont, Pathé, and Lumière in France; Edison, American Mutoscope & Biograph, and Vitagraph in New York. Perhaps I have overlooked a few, but the Méliès and Pathé companies were making the best foreign pictures and had a ready market here in the United States. Lumière and Pathé also manufactured cameras and tripods which were sold here. The products of both firms were compact, easy to handle and operate, while the cameras and tripods manufactured in the United States were custom built for each individual company and were heavy, bulky pieces of equipment. The first Biograph camera weighed so much that it took two men to lift it onto the tripod.

My first opportunity to operate a moving picture camera came when Lubin wanted me to photograph some titles to replace those in a French picture I had just finished duping. The big moment had arrived. Lubin unlocked the closet where the camera was kept under lock and key when not in use. In the spring of 1906 Edison had let it be known that anyone who used a moving picture camera that infringed on his U.S. patent would be prosecuted unless licensed by him. For this reason, the camera was always carefully locked up. Edison's patent covered the vital mechanical movement, including evenly spaced perforated sprocket holes in the film it used. Although Lubin was aware that Edison had engaged detectives to ferret out infringers, it didn't bother him in the slightest. He stepped into the closet, pointed to a huge, clumsy camera, and said, "There, see vat gutt titles you can make."

The camera was so heavy I had to get some help to carry it up the narrow staircase to the studio above and place it on the table used for making titles. The outside of the camera was made of highly polished mahogany, but, to my surprise, when I opened the door on the side, I found that the wood casing concealed a sheet-iron case. The mechanism was almost the duplicate of the printer I had been using to make dupes in the laboratory. The camera lacked a finder or optical system for viewing the aperture. In order to focus, it was necessary to lean sideways, poke your head inside the camera, and focus on the emulsion of the film. After threading and focusing the film, the side door was closed. The crank was just forward of the door hinges. At one end of the table was a framelike device for positioning the camera in its precise place.

My experience making lantern announcement slides for nickelodeons, such as, "Ladies, Please Remove Your Hats," certainly came in handy. I used positive instead of negative plates in the camera, and this produced a desirable strong black-and-white contrast. I threaded the movie camera with positive film and photographed the hand-lettered titles, and when the film was developed, it had that same rich contrast. When Lubin saw them, he raved, and wanted to know why he had never had such good titles before.

Only a few days later I was sent out to photograph scenes with Jack Frawley, the director. Usually, we put three subjects on a reel of about a thousand feet. We seldom made a picture over eight or nine hundred feet in length. Story ideas were concocted by Frawley and we made the pictures without benefit of a script. We didn't even number scenes as we photographed. Frawley would trust to memory and a few notes he had made on a scratch pad when the time came to cut and assemble a picture. Lengthy, descriptive titles had to be added to make the pictures understandable.

When I wasn't photographing, there were always dupes to be made, and I began to resent this, not because my conscience was bothering me, but because I believed we could make better pictures that the ones we duped. I had discovered that Lubin wasn't the only one who took part in the shady business of duping: it was common practice. Everybody was duping the best pictures made abroad and underselling one another. It seemed to me that the extra cost involved in making our own pictures could easily be made up by the increased sale of prints.

In my two years with Lubin, there is one incident I don't think I'll ever forget. He asked me to screen some pictures for a prospective buyer who didn't disclose his identity but said he was in the market to buy some films. As we sold to anyone who had the cash, Lubin hustled the customer into a small screening room where I was waiting to grind the projector, which was set up without a booth. After showing a few of the pictures made by Lubin without a sale, he had me run some dupes. Among them was *A Trip To The Moon,* one of Méliès best pictures. Practice had made me quite expert at blocking out the trademarks, and the job on this picture was so good it was hard for our customer to believe his eyes. Suddenly he jumped up from his chair, shot his arm out in front of the beam of light from the projector, and shouted, "Stop the machine." Startled, I stopped grinding and turned on the light. Lubin stared at him wondering what was wrong. We found out soon enough when the prospective buyer shouted, "You want me to buy that film?" Lubin wanted to know why not. "I," the man bellowed thumping his chest, "I made that picture. I am Georges Méliès from Paris." The man, quite naturally, was in a wild rage. Lubin glared at him and, pointing to me, brazenly began telling Méliès what a hard time I had had blocking out the trademark. Lubin's defiant attitude stunned Mr. Méliès, and he stood there speechless. Lubin seemed to consider the incident a joke, and I was dumbfounded when he went out laughing. I didn't see the humor of the situation as Méliès was in such a rage he could have become physically violent, but he soon stamped out of the room. After that, whenever I was asked to run dupes for prospective buyers I was always a bit fearful.

Besides duping and occasionally making a picture, we faked championship bouts by using matched doubles for the boxers and staging the round-by-round action from the newspaper accounts. We then sold the picture as the actual championship fight with the real boxers. We even made a one-reel picture portraying the shooting of Stanford White by Harry K. Thaw over the love of his wife, Evelyn Nesbit Thaw, on the night of January 26, 1906, at Madison Square Garden roof in New York City.

On April 18, 1906, when the news arrived of the great disaster that was the San Francisco earthquake and fire, Jack Frawley made a hasty trip to get some scenes of the smoking ruins. Home in our Philadelphia studio we staged tumbling buildings made from cardboard profiles, but even with the smoke that we used for effects and the silhouettes of the cardboard buildings, the scenes looked like fakes.

Edison detectives were having a hard time trying to come by substantial evidence of infringement of his patent that would stand up in court and, what made it worse, several small new companies now were in the business of making moving pictures. It became rather amusing, something like a game of hide-and-seek. When a company planned to work outdoors, they sent out a decoy group for the detectives to follow and spend the day watching, while the real shooting company left the studio later and worked unmolested all day. With the exception of the American Mutoscope & Biograph camera, there wasn't a moving picture camera in use in the United States at that time that didn't infringe on the Edison patents. The American Mutoscope & Biograph 35mm camera perforated two sprocket holes in each frame as it photographed, and therefore it did not use film that was perforated with evenly spaced sprocket holes as stipulated in the Edison patents. But it was probably the most cumbersome ever built to photograph 35mm film.

Although the patent situation was quite involved, I will try to simplify the complications. U.S. Patent Office records show that Thomas A. Edison applied for patents on a moving picture camera and a viewing device on August 24, 1891. The patent on the viewing device was granted in 1893, but the patent on the camera and perforated film that it used wasn't granted until August 31, 1897. These patents applied only to the United States. At approximately the same time (1894), the Lumière brothers of Lyons, France, came up with a moving picture camera that also was a printer and projector. In this instance, their patents covered only France. A third camera was developed in England and, again, the patent applied only in England. Even today the invention of the motion picture camera is claimed by several countries. With this background, it is easy to understand how this situation set the stage here in the United States for a free-for-all as to who had or had not the right to make moving pictures, with what camera, made in what country, and under what patents. Edison's demand for royalties brought a howl of protests and such accusations as, "He swiped the idea from the Lumière brothers in France," and "Weren't the Lumière brothers the first to show a picture on the screen?" All the charges and screaming accomplished nothing; Edison's patents were valid.

In October, 1907, things were slow with Lubin so I made a trip to New York to spend a little time with my parents. There were rumors that some of the companies, because of Edison's threat of a lawsuit, were going to make a deal with him to be licensed and pay royalties for the use of his patents. The independent exchange men took this as a move to monopolize the business and eliminate them. To insure against having their supply of pictures cut off, these men began making their own under cover.

I think Miles Brothers was the first exchange with the foresight to prepare themselves for what was to come. At that time, a cameraman who was a friend of mine, George Dobson, was working for them, photographing what today we call industrial films. He also photographed short subjects such as sporting events, political figures, and other items of national interest. The exchange rented these films to the nickelodeons to fill a bill, and, if the event was of great national importance, the film would become the main attraction and, as such, was advertised on the display out front. I ran into Dobson on Broadway and he filled me in on what had been happening in the picture business around New York. Dobson told me there were plenty of jobs as a lot of the exchanges were now in need of cameramen.

I liked living at home in New York and had begun to think that if I could land something worthwhile, I would consider moving. I had had enough of the duping business. Getting away from that would be my first consideration in changing jobs, so out of curiosity, I took Dobson's tip and went to talk with the men who operated the Mosher and Harrington film exchange. When Mosher heard that I had been with Lubin for two years, he wanted me to start right away. When he told me what the job would pay, I became suspicious and asked him point blank if he expected me to make dupes on the side. To my surprise his answer was no, so I took him up on his offer. On my way home I sent a telegram to the Lubin Manufacturing Company to let them know I wouldn't be back.

The next morning I showed up bright and early and Mr. Mosher handed me the Pathé field camera I was to use. It was much smaller than the camera at the Lubin Company. The main difference was that the Pathé was much lighter and therefore portable. Made of highly polished mahogany, the Pathé camera magazines held two hundred feet of film.

The mechanical movement, of course, was an infringement on the patents held by Edison.

My first Mosher and Harrington assignment was to photograph an industrial film for a company that manufactured kid gloves in the town of Gloversville in upstate New York. When that was finished I made some short subjects of a few political personalities at Tammany Hall in New York City. I worked freely with the camera in the open because none of the Edison snoopers bothered us when politicians were around.

Mr. Mosher told me my next job would be to photograph the start of President Theodore Roosevelt's sixteen-battleship cruise around the world which was scheduled to leave Hampton Roads, Virginia, on the morning of December 16, 1907. When I reached Hampton Roads, the first person I saw was George Dobson who had been sent on the same mission by the Miles Brothers. We both had instructions to try to make this event a special so it could be billed as a main attraction. Dobson and I got together with some newspaper photographers and hired a tugboat for the day. The sixteenth was a bright morning, and we sailed around the ships before they weighed anchor, photographing from all angles. Our tug kept ahead of the fleet as it left and started for the open sea, grinding away with our Pathé cameras while the others snapped still pictures until the tug began tossing about like an eggshell on the rough sea. A few of us turned somewhat green but the sight of those sixteen powerful battlewagons plowing through the sea toward us with the spray shooting high in the air and then passing us broadside as they headed for the blue sea beyond was truly an awe-inspiring sight.

When we returned to New York, I heard that Lubin, Vitagraph, Kalem, Selig, Essanay, George Kleine, and Pathé had all agreed to be licensed and to pay royalties for the use of the Edison patents. American Mutoscope & Biograph held out as their Biograph camera didn't infringe. I always have believed that this greedy little group, instead of creating a monopoly for themselves as intended, succeeded only in creating opposition from the exchange men who never before thought of making moving pictures but who now were forced to do so to protect themselves. Ironically, some of the exchange men were the very persons who led the fight that finally broke the trust which organized a year later and which harassed these little companies in every possible way for the next four or five years. The number of these small companies grew. They became known as independents and sometimes were called "blanket companies" from the practice of keeping a blanket over the camera in order to circumvent the Edison detectives. For further protection, most of them employed a rather husky individual whose job it was to stand near the camera and discourage anyone who was too curious.

What made the patent fight even more complicated and difficult to understand was that some of the companies that now paid royalties for the use of Edison patents discarded the bulky cameras they had built for themselves and began using the light, portable camera imported from France. The question was how could Edison dictate who in the United States should use a camera imported from France. Unless one were completely familiar with the entire patent situation, the question seemed logical.

Chapter 2

THE EARLY FILM COMPANIES CRESCENT AND BISON

I N THE SPRING of 1908 I began looking for a partner in order to form a company of my own to make moving pictures. I found the young man I was looking for in Herman Kolle. Although he knew nothing about making moving pictures, he was intrigued by the idea. His father owned Prospect Hall at 273 Prospect Avenue in South Brooklyn, New York. The hall had a good-sized dance floor, a balcony running around three sides of the place, and a stage at one end. Next to and in connection with the dance hall was an open air summer beer garden. On warm summer evenings neighborhood families would sit around at the separate tables, drink nickel schooners of beer, and watch second-rate vaudeville on a stage raised about seven feet above the ground. A screen rolled down from the arch over the stage and this was used to show movies. A song plugger sang popular tunes, accompanied by a piano, while the hand-colored lantern slides on the screen changed according to the lyrics of the song. There was only enough business to warrant opening on Saturday and Sunday evenings. If it rained, people would move into the dance hall and the show would continue there.

We used one corner of the summer garden for our open-air studio and, as in the early days of Lubin, daylight was our only source of light for photography. We arranged a tiny laboratory under the stage and bought a used Pathé field model camera that had seen better days. We also bought an old Powers projector head that had been converted into a step-printer (a device to print films frame by frame) with several rolls of perforated negative and positive film from Hans Schmidt, who ran a speakeasy-type movie equipment joint in the cellar of his house on Second Avenue in New York City.

Now we were ready to make moving pictures. We named our company the Crescent Film Company, and our trademark was a black crescent moon on a white background. Herman Obrock, the stage electrician at Prospect Hall who also ran the projecting machine in the evenings at the summer garden, spent a lot of time with us. He wanted to learn the business. He accompanied me to Coney Island the day I went there to photograph subjects I thought would make up a saleable reel. One subject was the shoot-the-chutes at Luna Park where a flat bottomed boat came down an incline through white bubbling water simulating rapids and made a big splash as it came to a stop in a large pool at the bottom, rather a spectacular scene. Another subject was the loop-the-loop on Surf Avenue. This was a wooden structure where an automobile

Fred J. Balshofer at about the time he founded the Crescent Film Company and was co-founder of the New York Motion Picture Company.

gained enough speed as it came down a steep incline to make an upside-down loop with two passengers in the auto. I had just finished cranking when we were spotted by the bouncers and.had to get out of there in a hurry.

We photographed scenes on the crowded Coney Island beach and scenes in Steeplechase Park. After shooting for two days, we ran out of film, so back we went to the summer garden to develop what we had photographed. This was the first film we developed in our little laboratory. Giving instructions to Kolle and Obrock, who helped, kept me hopping, and handling the heavy developing drums was by no means a one-man job. The next day I made nice, clean prints, rare in those days. When all the subjects were spliced together, there were two full reels of a thousand feet each.

Film exchange row was on Fourteenth Street in New York City, and with the reels under my arm, that's where I headed. First I called on the Empire Film Exchange, two doors west of Third Avenue on the south side of Fourteenth Street on the second floor. The exchange was owned by Adam Kessel and Charles Bauman. There was the usual counter where the operators from the nickelodeons brought back the reels of the program they had shown to exchange for other reels to make up their next program. Empire had a small office for the bosses and a still smaller screening room where they looked at pictures they might buy. Kessel and Bauman sat in the screening room with me as they watched the two reels I brought. We sat there in silence; the only sound was the clicking hum made by the projection machine. My apprehension grew. The lights were turned on but there was no discussion between the two men. Kessel seemed to be figuring everything out by himself. He turned, looked at me, and said, "If I buy five prints of each, will you give me an exclusive?" I replied I would have to think it over. "OK. We'll be outside. You take your time." The sale price of pictures at that time was ten cents a foot, so it was easy to figure a sale of this kind would give us a nice profit. I sat and stalled a little longer so I wouldn't appear too anxious. Then I went outside and agreed to the deal. Kessel asked me a few questions about my new company and said that he'd never heard of Crescent but that he would be interested in looking at the next pictures we made.

I promised to deliver the prints in a few days and left the place walking on air. When I told Kolle the news, he was elated too and immediately began talking about making moving pictures other than short subjects. Our next effort was a split reel. A split usually consisted of two separate comedies on one reel. We called one of our comedies *A Skate on Skates* and the other *Troublesome Baby.* Each was about three hundred and fifty feet in length. Our players could hardly be called actors as we used anyone we could pick up around the hall. The comedies didn't seem very funny to me, but they sold anyway.

Our little business was going along just fine when one pleasant afternoon a fellow came into the summer garden looking for me. He introduced himself as Al McCoy, said he represented the Edison Manufacturing Company, and wanted to see the camera we were using for making moving pictures. McCoy was a slim man of medium height in his mid-forties. I reminded him that he was trespassing on private property, and that if he didn't get out, I'd have him thrown out. I guess he believed I meant it for he left without making any trouble. McCoy didn't frighten me but I later noticed that Kolle was concerned. McCoy evidently never forgot our little encounter, for it was his persistent spying and harassment that caused the Crescent Film Company to dissolve a few months later.

I had an idea that western pictures were what the exchanges wanted, but we were in no financial position to compete with some of the westerns being produced, many of which cost up to fifteen hundred dollars apiece. As a way out, it occurred to me to make a western with teen-age youngsters, so I asked Kolle if he could gather about eight or ten boys from the neighborhood who would like to play in such a picture. He said he'd see what he could do. I gave Kolle a written outline of the story, and within a couple of days he was rehearsing some boys in the gymnasium of Prospect Hall. The picture was titled *Young Heroes of the West.*

When the day came to shoot the picture, eight teen-agers

gathered at the hall at eight o'clock in the morning. Some had their own costumes, while Kolle had rented others from an outfit that specialized in rentals for the masquerade balls that were popular in those days. All the boys had brought lunches and were a happy bunch of kids. I told them Kolle wasn't going to be there and introduced myself as the man who was going to make the picture. I took a good look around to be sure that Edison's private eye, McCoy, wasn't there spying, and then I carried the camera covered with a blanket while some of the boys grabbed the tripod and a leather case with some extra film magazines. We boarded a Fifth Avenue trolley car at the corner and headed for the location I had in mind, a golf course called Dyker Heights on 69th Street that was surrounded on three sides by wooded country, making it ideal for the background. Besides, it was quite secluded from prying eyes.

As we boarded the trolley, one youngster made it his business to sit beside me and began telling me about a Brownie box camera he used to make his own pictures. I gave yes and no answers to his questions about photography until he began interrogating me about the movie camera, still covered with a blanket, on the floor between my legs. I didn't know whether Kolle knew this lad or not, but I did know that McCoy would stop at nothing to find out what make of camera I was using. The boy followed one question with another. I sized him up and figured he was pretty smart for his age, about fourteen, and could be a spotter for McCoy.

When the trolley turned off Fifth Avenue onto 69th Street, we soon reached the golf course. We walked along the edge of the course until we found a good site among the trees. I started to set up the camera, but it was obvious that the same lad was trying to get a look at it, so I quickly threw the blanket over the camera. Only when I was actually grinding a scene did the blanket come off. I watched the youngster all afternoon, becoming completely convinced that he was more than just one of the kids playing in the picture. Sure enough, when we went home in the trolley, there he was right beside me again, but the camera, as before, was covered with the blanket. This time he wanted to know how we developed the long strip of film we used in the movie camera. I told him if he wanted to see how it was done, he could come to the summer garden that evening and watch.

Obrock had enough experience by now so that the two of us could handle the developing, but as soon as I reached Prospect Hall I called Kolle and asked him to come over. I thought we were in trouble with McCoy and while we ate supper I told him of my suspicions. Kolle didn't seem any more certain than I. We walked to the entrance of the garden, and there was the youngster waiting. The minute Kolle saw him, he began to laugh, for he thought that this was one of the funniest incidents he had ever experienced. Kolle told me he knew the youngster, who was one of the boys from the neighborhood.

We started to get ready in the laboratory, and the young fellow wanted to know if he could help. Now that I was sure he wasn't on McCoy's side, I gladly let him. At that time we used the drum system for developing the film, the same system we used when I was with Lubin. When we talked about making positive prints the next day, the kid wanted to know if he could be there to see how it was done. He reminded me so much of myself when I was about his age and had been stung by the photographic bug, I said he could join us. As I expected, he finally asked me for a job. In those days it was not uncommon for a boy of fourteen to start learning a trade. He told me that his name was Arthur Miller and that he lived about a block from the summer garden. Arthur wanted to learn all he could, he said, so he could be a cameraman, and it wasn't long before he was doing routine chores that made it easier for me when we were working in our tiny laboratory. Once he understood McCoy's business, he kept an eye open for him the same as the rest of us.

Our next picture, *What Poverty Leads To*, was too long, the subject drab and dull. In spite of these shortcomings, we came out all right on it. Then we made *Chaucey Proves A Good Detective*. This was an improvement. We even had two small interiors in the picture. Like other companies, our sets were an offspring of the theater. The walls were canvas flats about five feet wide and eleven feet high. The walls were held upright by stage braces as they were in the theater, while the edges were held together with clamps. After the flats were placed to form the desired room, a scenic artist painted the walls. His artistry added the mouldings, the door and window frames, and the landscape seen through the windows. Sometimes the wall fluttered a bit if the door was not closed gently. The nickelodeon audiences accepted all this. Very often they would hiss the villain and applaud the hero on the screen.

We covered the top of the set with lightweight muslin to diffuse the direct sunlight and used silverleaf reflectors to brighten up certain parts of the set. Usually the sets were laid out with the entrance door in the background which disclosed the full figure of the actor as he made an entrance. For the more important parts of the scene, the action was staged to

A typical open-air stage in a summer garden.

move the actors to the foreground, especially to register their spoken titles. An actor never came close enough to the camera to show more of his figure than from the knees up. This was known as an "American" foreground. The "French" foreground was when the camera cut in the middle of the shins.

For *What Poverty Leads To*, we used William Kolle, Herman's older brother. He was a good-looking man, six feet tall and well-proportioned, with a shock of red hair. William was in charge of Prospect Hall and the summer garden as the senior Kolle was getting on in years and semi-retired. William enjoyed playing in pictures, but the business of dodging McCoy, the detective, began to worry him. We had a little gate at the back of the garden, and when the signal sounded that McCoy had been seen, I would pick up the camera and tripod and make a dash for the gate that led into the hall through a rear entrance.

The next and last picture made by the Crescent Film Company was *A Desperate Character*. Again William Kolle played the lead. I noticed he had become very much concerned about McCoy. The situation really had upset him, and I guess he also felt the responsibility of the management of the hall and didn't want to be involved in any litigation. I never found out for sure, but I suspect he told Herman we would have to quit. At any rate, Herman talked to me and said he would take five hundred dollars for his share of what we owned. I said I would find someone to buy him out. McCoy didn't frighten me; I was in business to stay and really began to enjoy outwitting his snooping tactics.

Late in the fall of 1908, the news got around that Crescent was going out of business. Dave Horsley was just starting a small company called Centaur over in Bayonne, New Jersey. A year later it was known as the Nestor Company. Dave looked me up and suggested that I go in business with him. He was about thirty-eight, more than ten years my senior, and I felt he would make a good partner. He offered me fifty percent of the company without my putting up a dime, but he wasn't interested in buying out Kolle. Since I didn't want Kolle to lose money, I turned the deal down.

During the time I had been selling Crescent pictures to Kessel and Bauman, owners of the Empire Film Exchange, I had come to know some of the background of these two men, and it now occurred to me that they were the kind who didn't scare easily and who might be interested in going into a partnership. Both had been born in Brooklyn, each sported a moustache, but that's where any similarity ended. Adam Kessel was thirty-five, tall, slim, and wiry. He had been a bookmaker at the Jamaica, Sheepshead Bay, Brighton Beach, and Gravesend tracks, all of which were scattered around Brooklyn and Long Island. Kessel had been around and was no easy mark. Charlie Bauman was thirty-two, short, heavy set, with a dark complexion. A former streetcar conductor, he liked to boast of putting a nickel in his pocket out of every four fares he rang up. He also had been around and was nobody's chump. I still get a chuckle every time I hear the story repeated of how a director borrowed a diamond ring and deliberately flashed it in Addie Kessel's eye and bluffed him into paying a higher salary. Whoever originated this story couldn't have known Addie Kessel.

When we met in the office of their exchange on 14th Street, I no sooner spoke of a partnership than Kessel asked, "What's the deal?" I suggested that the two of them would be one partner, while I would be the other, with a split two ways. After much discussion, finally it was agreed that it would be a three-way split, share and share alike. They would pay Kolle his five hundred dollars as well as put up fifteen hundred dollars against my experience, and the new company would be known as the New York Motion Picture Company.

I paid off Kolle as promised and moved the few things we owned to a three-story loft building on 17th Street between 7th and 8th Avenues, Brooklyn, about a mile from the summer garden. There we occupied the top floor. The two sky-lights in the roof made the place light and cheerful. Arthur had been paying attention to his work and had learned my way of doing things, so I took him with me. Our new laboratory had a good deal more space, which meant we could handle a larger quantity of film. We had two step-printers and several

Miller judging printing light from test strip in the New York Motion Picture Company's laboratory on 17th Street, Brooklyn, New York, in 1909.

more drums and tanks for developing and were now equipped
to do much more dye-toning and tinting of positive film which
had become quite popular.

Early in 1909 our company was incorporated officially as
the New York Motion Picture Company with a capital of
$10,000. The par value of the stock was $100 a share. As
agreed, we split the stock three ways, giving the odd share
to Miss May Kenny, business secretary of their exchange, who
was going to serve also as the secretary of our newly formed
company. Adam Kessel was president, Charles Bauman was
vice-president, and I was secretary-treasurer as well as general
manager in charge of picture making. Louis Burston, a lawyer
and a friend of both Kessel and Bauman, drew up the incorporation papers. He was to act as our legal advisor and was
given a few shares by Kessel and Bauman out of their stock.
He returned the stock in a few weeks for cash because he
didn't think we'd succeed and was absolutely certain the
stock never would be worth a dime.

In December, 1908, American Mutoscope & Biograph Company (generally called the Biograph) had gone in with those
who already were paying royalties for the use of the Edison
patents. The other companies, as mentioned earlier, were
Edison, Vitagraph, Selig, Kalem, Lubin, Essanay, Pathé, and
George Kleine. All of these companies now officially announced the formation of a new organization called the Motion Picture Patents Company in January, 1909. Their plan
was to stop anyone outside of their trust from making moving
pictures in the United States. However, they didn't take into
account an old saying to the effect that the best laid plans
of mice and men often go astray. The announcement of the
Patents Company was tantamount to a declaration of war on
the independents. The Patents Company's next move was to
contract with the Eastman company to buy Eastman's entire
United States output of perforated film as a move to protect
their monopoly.

Adam Kessel took this to be the first shot fired in their
declared war and reacted as I expected he would. We had a
session at Mouquin's French Restaurant on Sixth Avenue and
28th Street. Seated around the table were Charles and Addie

Kessel, Charles Bauman, and me. The minute the talk started, I could tell I had not misjudged my partners, for, as I had figured, Addie Kessel was full of fight. To counteract the Eastman deal with the trust, it was decided that the next day I would see Jules Brulatour, the New York importer of Lumière film manufactured in France, to make arrangements for our supply of film, as well as to make inquiries about having the film perforated. After our plans were set, we had our dinner, and somehow it seemed as if we were celebrating a victory. When the waiter brought the check on a small plate, Charlie Kessel placed a ten-dollar bill on it. As he did so, his eye caught the picture of a buffalo on the bill. With a smile he pushed the plate toward the center of the table and said, "Here's a good trademark for your company. It will fit right in with your western pictures." Addie thought it looked pretty good, but didn't think Buffalo Pictures sounded quite right. The waiter standing by spoke up and said, "They call those animals bison too." So Bison became the name and trademark of our company.

The next day I went to see Eberhard Schneider who had an optical store on East 12th Street where he sold movie equipment that he had designed and built himself. Fortunately, he could let me have one of his perforators immediately, and he agreed to deliver a second one as soon as possible. We placed the first perforator on the bench in the printing room and arranged to run it slower than the recommended speed as a precaution against static. As well as being my camera boy, it became young Miller's job to carefully perforate the supply of negative film on days when there was no photographing to be done.

It was now about the middle of March and, although the weather was still a bit cold, we decided to make our first picture. From the beginning I had wanted to make westerns, which meant that our locations would be across the Hudson River in and around Fort Lee and Coytesville, New Jersey. Most of the trust and independent companies worked there and it was ideal for westerns. I knew, though, that it meant trouble as the trust had their spies on the job.

Both Kessel and Bauman thought it wise to make a few pictures as far away from the Patents Company's spotters as possible. They felt that this would give us a chance to assemble a small company as well as time to make certain that when we were set we would have people we could rely upon for our entry into the lion's den in Jersey. Some of the independents already were working over there, despite the continued harassment by the Patents Company. I agreed with my partners that this was the only solution.

Two or three weeks prior to our decision to make a few pictures quietly, a young fellow dropped in at the Brooklyn laboratory. He was a good-looking chap, about thirty years of age. He had written a story called *Disinherited Son's Loyalty*, and he said that if I gave him the leading role in the movie, the story would be mine for nothing. The young man claimed to have had experience playing small parts in a stock company in a downtown Brooklyn theater. The day we started the picture, however, I could tell at once that he had never put on greasepaint makeup in his life. This was part of the actor's profession, as makeup men were unheard of at that time. As an actor, he turned out to be as phony as one historian's tale to the effect that Adam Kessel and Charlie Bauman appeared as actors in this picture.

This incident decided us that from now on we would make use of experienced actors wherever possible. I was acquainted with a young actor, Charles French, who had worked for the Biograph on and off. For our second picture, I made a deal with him to play the leading male role as well as to help direct. For our leading lady, we selected Evelyn Graham, a stage actress. We made the picture around the waterfront at Sheepshead Bay in Brooklyn and called it *A Fisherman's Romance*. It was while making this picture that I began to take staging and directing seriously. I had been watching young Miller's progress with the camera as I had become fond of the youngster. I had taught him to grind at the correct speed, and he could thread a camera without any trouble. His one problem was that he was small for his age, and I realized that when the time came for him to grind the camera, he'd have to stand on a box to reach it.

A *Fisherman's Romance* was a great improvement over our first picture; they both ran a little over eight hundred feet. The next story I bought from Charlie French for ten dollars was called *Davy Crockett in Hearts United*. Here again the same historian made an actor of Adam Kessel, for he reports Kessel took the part of Davy Crockett. Actually, Charlie French was Davy with Evelyn Graham as his leading lady. What the historian didn't report was that Charlie Bauman, who had never before acted, played the girl's father. It was Bauman's first and last appearance as a motion picture actor.

The Davy Crockett picture called for wild, virgin country-side so the company crossed the Hudson on the 42nd Street Ferry, hired a horse-drawn rig called a stage to drive us to the location in the woods between the towns of Palisades and Fort Lee, New Jersey. Here we found a picturesque road through the woods that paralleled what is now Anderson Avenue. The first day we drove over to Pete Cella's hotel for lunch. Cella's hotel was about a quarter of a mile from Main Street in Fort Lee, at that time a small, rural town with a dusty, unpaved dirt street. A horse-drawn water wagon with two sprinklers at the rear laid the dust twice a day. In the middle of the road was a single trolley track with a siding at intervals to allow a trolley going in one direction to switch off and let a trolley headed in the opposite direction pass. On either side of the street were large telegraph poles with dozens of wires stretched from one to the other.

After lunch, not far from the hotel, I found just the mansion we had in mind as the residence of the girl and her wealthy father. The people in Fort Lee were accustomed to the movie companies using their homes (for a small fee, of course), so we made arrangements to work around the house the next day. We shot some more scenes in the woods the following morning and, after lunch, moved to shoot the last scene at the mansion. This scene required Bauman, as the father, to walk from the background to join his daughter and a dressed-up eastern dude who was waiting with the parson for Bauman to give his daughter's hand in marriage. The daughter, according to the script, did not love the dude. She loved Davy Crockett who came charging by on horseback in the nick of time to sweep the girl off her feet and ride away. Ladies were a little more plump in those days and Charlie French had one hard time trying to accomplish this bit of heroism. The scene ended with Davy riding his horse holding the heroine's hand as she ran alongside until they were out of camera range. The next and last scene was played in front of Davy's cabin in the woods, where the minister performed the wedding ceremony while Davy delivered his spoken title, "Mother, I have brought you a daughter."

Davy Crockett was the type of picture we had decided we would make when we formed the Bison Company, and the sale of prints proved how right our judgment was. Our next film was *A Squaw's Revenge*, followed by a split-reel with one picture a comedy and the other a drama. The number of prints sold of the split-reel decreased substantially and forced us to the conclusion that if we were going to succeed as film-makers, we would have to take the final step in defiance of the trust and make only westerns, which meant we would have to work exclusively around Fort Lee and Coytesville, New Jersey. Both Kessel and Bauman agreed that now was the time to sink or swim.

We had acquired a story with the unlikely name of *The True Heart of An Indian* and had hired an actor, who also had done some work with the Biograph, to play the Indian character lead. The actor was to help in directing the picture, too. Our favorite historian says the actor in question was Charles French, but this is incorrect, for it was Charles Inslee, who wore a black wig parted in the center with two braids that reached below his shoulders. He was costumed in a breech-cloth, giving him an excellent opportunity to display his fine physique. Again we used Evelyn Graham as the leading lady, and for realism and color, we added two authentic Indians to the cast, Young Deer and his wife Red Wing.

We followed the practice of the other independents and employed a tough-looking fellow named Al Richard whom Kessel found for us through some old bookmaker friends. Richard weighed close to 225 pounds, stood over six feet tall, and at first glance looked very much like a prizefighter. His job was to stand by the camera to discourage anyone from getting too close.

The day before we were to start the new picture, I went to the laboratory in Brooklyn, told young Miller to meet me at the New York side of the Fort Lee Ferry at 125th Street early the next morning, and told him to bring four loaded camera magazines with him. The hiding place of the camera itself was always my secret and responsibility.

Charles Inslee in *The True Heart of An Indian*, made by Fred Balshofer for Bison brand pictures in Coytesville, New Jersey, in 1909.

Chapter *3*

MAKING *THE TRUE HEART OF AN INDIAN*

A T THE LABORATORY the next morning I loaded the four camera magazines as instructed and took one extra roll in a can to be on the safe side. We had a stock of Lumière film that came in 60-meter rolls (about 180 feet). It was early and nobody had yet arrived at the lab so I left a note for George Lane, the accountant, to let him know I had gone. The trip to the 125th Street ferry house took a little over an hour.

The New York Motion Picture Company had prospered. Fred was waiting and waved me into an auto he was driving. Beside him was a pretty tough-looking character, and I presumed he was the fellow who was going to stand by the camera in case we had trouble with the trust's detectives. He looked like he was well-qualified for the job. The tripod was lying on the floor in the back of the auto, and the camera was up front, well covered. Fred drove on the ferry boat in line with the other cars and when we landed at Edgewater, on the Jersey side, it looked like another world to me. Separated from the busy city of New York by the Hudson River, we were at the foot of the high cliffs of the Palisades. We drove along the river road, well shaded by trees, for about three miles. Then began the steep climb up the Palisades, and, as the road neared the top, the grade was so steep the car barely made it. As we leveled off, at the crest, we looked straight down Main Street, Fort Lee.

Main Street.
Fort Lee, New Jersey,
the first American
movie capital.

It certainly never occured to any of us that this small rural
town would soon become the movie capital of the world, years
before Hollywood, California, gained that title. The trolley
tracks from the ferry joined Main Street, a little beyond the
top of the hill, and about four blocks farther we turned onto
Fourth Street, now called Lemoyne Avenue, and drove through
the woods to Coytesville, a little over a mile up the river, and
two miles west from the cliffs of the Palisades. Coytesville was
sparsely populated, but there were tree-lined dirt roads, and
steep, wooded hills and forests. First Street was perhaps a mile
long, and about halfway was Rambo's roadhouse and saloon.
Rambo's is a landmark and a historic spot of the early movie-
making days. The saloon then was a two-story frame building
with a wooden front porch topped by a steep, slanted roof.
There were no poles or wires to spoil photographing from any
direction, and the dirt road Rambo's faced had a typical western appearance. Many a pair of ugly cowboys stepped out the
front door of Rambo's Saloon and squared off on the dusty road
for a shoot out. This was also the place where the stagecoach
picked up passengers and reported the holdup to the sheriff
who immediately formed a posse and started the chase of the
bandits. Within a stone's throw was a tree where each day at
least one bad man finished his life dangling from the end of a
rope.

Rambo's Hotel
in Coytesville
about 1907.

The second floor of this now historic place was used as dressing rooms for most of those who became the early stars of the motion picture business. At the back of the saloon was a cistern with a pump where the "Indians" washed the Bole Armenia or reddish water paint from their bodies after a hard day's work. Any morning the sun shone there would be extras waiting at Rambo's hoping to be chosen by one of the different companies that came to Coytesville.

On the street in back of the saloon was Capt. Anderson's livery stable where the companies rented their horses, western saddles, cowboy chaps, and whatever else it took to make a cowboy. When we arrived, Charlie Inslee was waiting for us in front of the stable, and the rest of the company, including a couple of extras all done up as cowboys and mounted on rented horses, ready to go. Our two cars drove slowly, the extras following on horses, and a short distance down the road we shot the first scene. Since it was our first day, things didn't go as smoothly as Fred would have liked them to. Having Charlie Inslee play the character lead as well as help direct naturally slowed things down a bit. The transition from stage technique to broad pantomime that Inslee insisted upon was difficult for Miss Graham. Fred Balshofer, always conscious of the final effect, was anxious to select pleasing compositions, so he insisted that western pictures, to be successful, must consist of a series of beautiful pictures combined with fast-moving action to tell a story, with as few subtitles as possible. He felt that at the end of the picture the villain should get the worst of it while the hero got the girl. Inslee, as an actor first and a director second, took a lot of convincing, but finally agreed.

The camera never moved during the taking of a scene. The actors played their scenes within a predetermined area that was marked off by stretching sash cord from wooden pegs that were driven in the ground. It was the director's job to see that the actors played within the confines of the marked area. The

Evelyn Graham in the center. Young Deer and his wife, Red Wing, on the right. Red Wing built the teepee according to Indian tradition. Photographed in Coytesville, New Jersey in 1909.

mild friction at the start wasn't helped by the ever-present worry of having the Patents Company's snooper appear on the scene. We had moved to three or four locations to shoot scenes by the time the lunch hour came around. After packing up, we drove back to the livery stable, where Fred stashed away the camera, and we all walked over to Rambo's for lunch.

At one side of the hotel was a grape arbor, at least one hundred feet long. Underneath it was a planked table which ran the full length, with benches on both sides. Several other companies were already seated along the table having lunch, and several people greeted Fred Balshofer and Charlie Inslee. The only food ever served at Rambo's was ham and eggs, bread and butter, coffee and homemade apple pie. The experience of sitting under the grape arbor with actors, directors, and cameramen and hearing them swap stories, gossip and ideas was delightful, and was something I enjoyed for the next few years. Both trust and independent companies met there on the most friendly terms. It seemed to me that the only ones who wanted to cause trouble were the detectives hired by the trust and, particularly, their head man, Al "Slim" McCoy.

I don't think I'll ever forget when Fred introduced Billy Bitzer, then with the Biograph, to me as "the best cameraman in the business." I listened but I couldn't believe that anyone was a better cameraman than Fred Balshofer. But, years later, when I saw *Birth of A Nation, Way Down East,* and *Broken Blossoms,* I at last realized how great Bitzer was. I remember that once he showed Fred a special magnifying glass he had placed in the long focusing tube of his camera. Bitzer told Fred the name of the shop where he could have his camera altered. Fred took his advice and claimed that the new magnifying tube helped to make the pictures he photographed much sharper in focus.

We finished our lunch and went back to work until midafternoon when it started to cloud over. While we were working, I don't think I ever took my eyes off the camera and what Fred was doing. During waiting periods there was time enough for me to ask questions. Sometimes Fred moved the camera a few inches one way and then moved it again before he decided just where the camera should be placed to shoot the scene. When I asked him for an explanation, he told me to remember always that there was a particular spot that would produce the best composition. He would expound at length as to how the clearness of the sky and whether the background was light or dark determined the exposure, and the direction of the sun was best when it came from three-quarters front. This, he said, gave perspective to photography.

As I look back on those formative years, I realize how extremely fortunate I was to have had such an instructor. After waiting awhile that afternoon for the sun, Fred gave up, and we quit for the day. Fred, Al Richard, and I drove to the laboratory in Brooklyn. During the return ride I began to like Richard, for he didn't seem like such a tough customer after all. Actually, he turned out to be a gentle sort of man, and when I learned he lived in Brooklyn not far from the lab, I liked him even more. He stayed at the laboratory and watched while Fred developed the negative and soon was hooked by pho-

Crew of the New York Motion Picture Laboratory: BACK ROW: *second from left*, Al Richard; *center*, George Lane, bookkeeper; *extreme right*, Walter Walters, printer. SEATED: *at left*, Reinhard, negative developer, *third from left*, Charlie Kipper, all-around lab man; *fourth*, Jack Gill, positive developer; *fifth*, Arthur Miller and, *at extreme right*, Mr. Lamphier, the chemist.

tography. Fred was pleased with the result of the developed negative. The use of exposure meters, machine developing, and the perfection of film processing today, all make it hard to understand the satisfaction and pleasure experienced in those days when you were sure that what you had spent the day photographing had turned out satisfactorily.

On the second and last day of the picture, we had no sooner arrived to pick up the horses at the livery stable than Fred was tipped off that McCoy of the Patents Company was in town. We had built a small, slab log cabin deep in the woods in a clearing, on the theory that this was too far away to be easily detected. We worked around it all morning. After lunch the picture was finished except for one scene where the cabin was to catch fire and Red Wing was to run in and rescue Miss Graham, who was supposed to be overcome by smoke. All day each of us had his attention diverted by trying to be on the lookout for McCoy. As a consequence, when the prop man prepared the cabin for the fire, no one paid much attention to what he was doing. When everything was in readiness, it somehow seemed a better idea not to put Miss Graham inside the cabin before starting the fire. Instead it was decided to have her wait outside until the right amount of fire was burning, then run in and close the door. Fred was to start turning the camera; Red Wing was to dash into the burning cabin, open the door, and help Miss Graham to safety. Both girls took their places on the sidelines close to the corner of the cabin. Inslee, who stood beside the camera some distance away, gave the prop man the signal to toss in the lighted piece of paper. As soon as the burning paper reached the cabin there was a tremendous explosion as the whole cabin burst into flames. The heat was unbearable. Both Fred and Inslee ran to the aid of the girls under the impression that both must have been injured. Luckily, both Red Wing and Miss Graham had had enough presence of mind to cover their faces and back off from the fire. I thought the camera was lost as the intense heat stopped anyone from approaching it. Al Richard, blanket in front of him like a shield, moved in and carried off the camera to safety. Nobody was aware that the prop man had literally soaked the slabs of the cabin with kerosene. Needless to say, that was the end of the day as well as of that prop man.

The girls were rushed by automobile to Rambo's, where first aid was administered at once. The news traveled fast. Some of the people around Rambo's were talking about what happened when, of all things, Fred Balshofer and Slim McCoy met face to face. Not a word was spoken. They just hesitated a moment, then passed one another. This was the first encounter since that day at the Crescent Film Company in the summer garden in Brooklyn. I pointed out McCoy to Al Richard, who was not impressed.

Fred had the front of the cabin rebuilt and shot the fire scene again with much more precaution. That finished the picture. Al Richard now worked in the lab any time we weren't out photographing. Fred cut the first print. It was then decided what scenes should be dye-toned or tinted.

Chapter 4

PATENTS COMPANY TROUBLES AND THE
DECISION TO MOVE WEST

K ESSEL AND BAUMAN were so delighted with the financial results of *The True Heart of An Indian* that we cele-brated by declaring a dividend. Our success, unfortu-nately, was also recognized by the trust, and although other independents had their troubles, we seemed to be the main target. McCoy and his cohorts appeared every place we went to photograph around Coytesville. Some in our company would spot one of the spies approaching and give me the signal. I folded the legs of the tripod, put the camera over my shoulder, and took off down the road or into the woods. When the de-tective reached Al Richard, who always remained behind, he usually suffered a change of heart and started back to where he came from. At no time did a situation arise where Richard had to use any strong-arm stuff, but the continued nuisance had the effect of making it impossible to work since all of us had become too jittery to concentrate.

When Jules Brulatour brought a camera built especially for the independents by Lumière from France, there seemed to be a ray of hope. The camera did not infringe on any of the Edison patents because it had no sprocket wheels, cam wheel, or teeth to engage the holes in the film to pull or jerk it into place at the aperture. It didn't require perforated film, the Latham loop, nor any kind of a loop to operate, but had a series of rollers to guide the film and a metal wheel with a flat section on it that took the place of a cam wheel to produce the necessary intermittent motion. The metal wheel was directly below the photographing aperture, and as there was no loop, the film had a strong tension between the feeder and the take-up magazines. When the camera was operated, the flat section of the wheel acted the same as a cam movement by knocking or pulling the film down into place at the aperture. The camera was turned over to me, and after shooting several scenes with it and doing everything I could to make it work, the camera simply proved to be no good. The film buckled continually, and when projected, it all but jumped off the screen. Our high hopes of telling Edison and the movie trust to go where we thought they ought came to naught.

The towns of Fort Lee and Coytesville were so small it was a cinch for McCoy and his added assistants to hound us. Now that the French camera was a bust, they bore down harder than ever. That forced us to do something about it, so

Charles French at left with Evelyn Graham. Man at right unidentified. Bison picture made in 1909 in Neversink, New York.

in the summer of 1909 we sneaked out of New York City up to the small town of Neversink in the Catskill Mountains. Our company consisted of Charlie French, Evelyn Graham, Young Deer and his wife Red Wing, J. Barney Sherry, Eddie Dillon, Charlie Inslee,. Bill Edwards our property man, Arthur Miller and me. Inslee again was cast as an Indian. Often just Inslee, Arthur, and I would pack off some distance to remote locations to get scenes of the lone Indian as he dodged around boulders and swam across streams busily tracking down the enemy for the white man, or as he arrived just in time to save a child or a fair maiden in distress. On these occasions, Arthur cranked the camera and learned more about composition and calculating exposure. Inslee made a striking appearance on the screen, and the ladies simply went gaga over him. Oh's and ah's came from them whenever he appeared on the screen in one of his naked Indian hero roles, so naturally most of his pictures were on that order. The names of the players did not appear on the film but Inslee had a flock of fans anyway, with letters coming to him through our New York office addressed to "The Indian," "The Lone Indian," and so on. Since he was human, these letters caused him to throw his chest out even further than he did in his moving picture roles.

At Neversink we lived in a large, broken-down boardinghouse and fixed up the side of a barn for use as our interiors when needed. We hired local residents as extras, turning them into cowboys or Indians by the use of makeup. The imposing Catskill mountain scenery, with cowboys and Indians riding like the wind over hill and dale and splashing through streams, combined with the clear mountain air, made it possible to get sharp, brilliant photography, which boosted the sale of the Bison films but also kept us the main target of the Patents Company. Try as he would, McCoy never learned where we had gone. We remained at Neversink until the snow began to fly; then we returned to New York.

Meanwhile, the Patents Company had put the bite on owners of nickelodeons, claiming that all the projecting machines used the same mechanical movement as the camera on which they held their patents. This intensified the campaign by the independents against the trust, and their series of cartoons in the *Moving Picture World,* the trade paper of the day, became more vicious. This time the Patents Company bit off more than they could chew, as most of the nickelodeon owners refused to kick in. In time the Patents Company abandoned the idea because it would have taken a small army to enforce their demands.

But they kept right on harassing the film-makers in an effort to put the independents out of business. McCoy was hot on our trail the minute we returned from Neversink. We tried to shoot a few scenes to finish a picture begun at Neversink, but it was the same old merry-go-round again.

Los Angeles with its mild climate and sunshine beckoned as an escape both from the winter months of the East as well as the ever-present Patents Company detectives. Late in November, 1909, found our little company of players, with the exception of Eddie Dillon, who had returned to the Biograph, and Arthur Miller, departing for the West Coast. Miller was heartbroken at his parents' objection to his leaving home. That he was a good boy, bright and ambitious as well as honest, raced through my mind, and it dawned on me that he would be hard to replace. I told him how sorry I was, for I had planned on his being my cameraman in California. "Honestly?" he asked, as tears started to form in his eyes.

My friend, Ed Porter, had been talking about starting a company of his own, so I sat down and wrote him a note about Arthur. Then I tried to cheer Arthur up by saying kiddingly, "From now on you'll have to keep your artistic eye open," which brought a faint smile as I handed him the sealed envelope. He stood there looking at me and extended his hand to say goodbye. As I said goodbye, too, I added, "Write and let me know how you make out with Porter." Arthur didn't answer but turned quickly and hurried away. I never realized until that moment just how fond of him I had grown. Replacing Arthur was a hurry-up affair. I can't remember now who recommended a young fellow named Maxwell Smith but hiring him was a big mistake as he proved to be an informer for the Patents Company.

Those of us who were leaving assembled at a downtown ferry and crossed the Hudson to New Jersey, where we were to board the Black Diamond express for Chicago, the first leg of our journey. I can't say I was surprised when I saw Arthur waiting on the platform. He came running toward me and was in good spirits. He had come over just to see me off. It was a bit hard for me to conceal my feelings, so I gave him a pep talk. "Arthur," I said, "You might have your ups and downs, but remember what you often have heard me say—nothing is impossible. Keep that in mind and some day you are going to be a fine cameraman." The others had boarded the train, and when I shook Arthur's hand, I could see he was over the disappointment of not going with us.

Chapter 5

WORKING FOR EDWIN S. PORTER

THE PLACE TO FIND OUT where any studio was setting up was at Eberhard Schneider's store and shop on east Twelfth Street, in New York City. Eberhard Schneider was a kindly German, probably in his fifties, and I was impressed when I saw the gold ring he wore in each ear. He always was ready and eager to answer questions concerning making moving pictures. Schneider had designed and built perforators, printers, and even a camera, in addition to many other gadgets. In one room of his building, he had a young man perforating film for the independents, and he also was equipped to develop small quantities of film using the drum system. I asked Mr. Schneider if he knew where I could find Mr. Porter, who was starting a new company. He told me that the studio was on Eleventh Avenue, between 41st and 42nd streets, and that he had just sold a perforator to the new company.

It didn't take me long to locate the loft building on the west side of Eleventh Avenue. The studio was on the second floor, where several workmen, carpenters, and painters were busy getting the studio ready. I approached one man who was connecting a cable to a bank of Cooper-Hewitt lights and asked him if he could tell me where I might find Mr. Porter. "I am Mr. Porter. What is it you want?" he inquired, with his attention still on the piece of equipment he was holding in his hand. I handed him Fred Balshofer's letter, and, after reading it, he looked at me and, rather disbelievingly said, "You look a little young to be a cameraman." I had no idea what Fred had written, but later I found out that he had said I would make a good cameraman. Porter's next question was whether I knew how to develop film. When I said "Yes," it seemed as if this moment was the first time he had paid any attention to me. The back part of the place had been partitioned off, and we entered through a zigzagging hall or light trap that made it possible to enter the dark rooms without using a door. Here was the fully equipped laboratory. To my surprise, the lab had a rack and tank system with which I was unfamiliar. Porter pointed to a can of film lying on a bench and with what sounded like a dare said, "Develop that roll of positive and call me when it's in the wash." With that, he pointed to a tank, saying, "That's the positive developer," and left the room. This abrupt manner, I learned by working with him for almost three years, was characteristic of the man and not an attitude.

After looking around at the equipment, it wasn't hard to figure out how to use the system. The developing racks, with pegs to space out the film as it was wound on, and the wooden stand to place the rack in, so that it turned while wrapping the film on, made it simple to understand. I darkened the room and lit the somewhat orange-colored light used when working with positive film instead of the ruby red light used for handling negatives. When the film was developed, fixed, and in the wash tank, I saw the film was a test to be used for making the different printing light numbers intended for use with the Houseman step-printer fastened to the bench. In those days, the printer did not have a light built in to make changes in printing light brightness to accommodate different densities of negatives. The apparatus used for the printing light was optional. Usually, though, as in this case, a hole was cut through the darkroom wall, through which a stick could slide. On the outside end of the stick was a Welsbach gas mantle that was excellent for printing since it produced a bright, white light. On the bench inside the darkroom were two side supports to keep the stick in a straight line when the mantle was moved to and from the aperture of the printer, thus increasing or decreasing the density of light as required.

I went out to the studio but couldn't find Mr. Porter, so I stuck my head in a small office and asked the man sitting at the desk to tell Porter the film was in the wash tank. "Mr. Porter has gone for the day," he said. "My name is Joe Engel. I'm Mr. Porter's partner so just hang the rack up to dry and he will look at it in the morning." I asked him if I should come back the next day. Mr. Engel replied, "Sure, Mr. Porter will want to talk to you."

I was already at the studio when Mr. Porter arrived the next morning. He handed me a large, wrapped sheet of cardboard to hold while he unlocked the door, and as soon as we entered he unfolded it and rested it against the wall to admire. It was a painting in black and white of an artillery type cannon, with smoke and fire belching from the barrel. Porter spoke gently, his abruptness gone, and said, "Don't you think that's a good trademark?" Underneath the picture was the word Defender. This was the name of his new company, and the cannon was his trademark. I reminded him of the film I had developed the day before and, with his mind evidently lingering on the trademark, we went into the darkroom. I was surprised to find the film had been removed from the rack, but he walked directly to where it was in a roll on the bench beside the printer. He gave no explanation as to how it had gotten there but held it in his hand and asked "Do you know what this film is for?" I told him I did.

Porter opened the door of a small locker and proceeded to change his clothes. "You had better bring some work clothes. We won't be making pictures until we get the place fixed up," he said. As soon as he was dressed, he began making the hole through the wall to put in the printing light. I helped him as much as I could, doing the carpenter work. He sent me out to buy some four-inch Welsbach gas mantles that we used for the printing light, and by the end of the day the job was finished. The more I worked while the studio was being set up, the more I realized that Ed Porter was a pretty thorough mechanic and that it was the mechanical aspect of filmmaking that interested him the most.

When the studio was ready to make pictures, it was equipped with Cooper-Hewitt lights only. The first thing I photo-

graphed in the studio was about fifty feet of film of the trademark. This I did one afternoon after Porter left and I was
sure he was putting me to a test. The camera was a Pathé, and
since I was alone I had the chance to make hand tests. I had
every opportunity to do a good job. By the time Porter arrived
the next day, I already had made the positive print of the
trademark. When he looked at the film, he was pleased and
mumbled, "Looks fine, looks fine." Mr. Porter seemed to soften
up, or I began to see him in a different light when he talked
about Fred Balshofer. He said that he heard that Fred was
going to make his pictures in California in the wintertime only
and would be back in the spring. This perked me up. As I
spent more time at the Defender studio, I began to appreciate
the time and patience that Fred had devoted to teaching me
about the laboratory and how to use a camera.

It was Joe Engel who actually hired me. I found out that
Porter took many things for granted, and very often when
talking to him about something, he seemed to be thinking about
another matter entirely. The puttering around and fixing up
of the studio went on until the beginning of April, 1910, when
a set was built. It was planned to photograph most of the
first picture inside the studio. Porter asked me if I was acquainted with one or two persons who knew the laboratory
business and who could be trusted. I immediately thought of
Al Richard, who was still at the laboratory in Brooklyn. Richard
had become quite expert at tinting and dye-toning the positive
prints different colors and combinations by toning one color
and tinting another over it. This was a must for every film
producer, and the trust and the independent companies alike
were doing it. After talking with Joe Engel, Al Richard decided
to come to work for Defender. One other fellow made up the
laboratory crew.

Our first movie was called something like *Russia, Country
of Depression,* and the only exterior scenes in the picture
were shot on Staten Island. Those scenes showed Russian Cossacks riding full speed through the countryside in search of
peasant cabins. The alarm shown by the peasants inside the
cabins, or sometimes a spoken title mentioning their fear of

the Cossacks at the door, was a trick used to avoid the necessity of building a cabin outside. Sometimes the peasant would open the door fearfully; if not, it would be broken down. Once inside the cabin, the Cossacks would beat the peasants with their whips and depart. We changed the dressing of the set and used different actors to make it appear that the Cossacks had visited several cabins. It was a horrifying subject for a picture and the expectation that fast-riding Cossacks would create the same colorful excitement as cowboys and Indians did not materialize. Hence the picture had a disappointing lack of success.

In a few weeks we made the second picture, a comedy, called *Too Many Girls*. The story was about a young ladies' finishing school where two girls fell for the same Dapper Dan. This brought about a mixed-up comedy chase, ending when the two girls doused each other in a lake. Again Porter chose Staten Island for the location. The Edison company had worked there frequently when he was with them, so I thought it natural for him to continue going over there instead of to New Jersey. Some time later I found out, however, that Porter was a wise little fox, for while McCoy and his gang were busy in Fort Lee, Porter was free to work without interference in Staten Island.

Our set in the studio was so designed that the flats could be changed to make several rooms simply by changing the accessories for each room. Using Cooper-Hewitt lights for photographing wasn't much of a challenge, for once you knew the amount of light needed to get the proper exposure, it was simple to place the banks of lights around the set and then photograph. There was no such thing as modeling, as the Cooper-Hewitt light was a mercury tube similar to the neon lights of today. It gave off a rather greenish-blue diffused light, so the pictures turned out flat without any gradations. Dye-toning and tinting added color to furnish somewhat of a contrast. Defender pictures were released through the Motion Picture Distributor and Sales Company, the first one in June, 1910. One picture was made each week until the end of the year, and that was when Defender came to an end.

I had been corresponding with Fred Balshofer in Los Angeles and from the tone of his letters, it was obvious that if there ever had been any hope that the Bison company might return to New York it had vanished. Each succeeding letter from Fred gave more reasons why Los Angeles was the place to make western pictures. Fred wrote about the nearby desert, the mountains, and he never failed to mention the continuous sunshine. Later on he began to tell me of the progress of a young fellow named Robert Newhard he was breaking in as a cameraman. The young man Fred had brought from New York as a replacement for me, Maxwell Smith, had been let go after some trouble.

In New York Ed Porter had formed a new company with Joe Engel and a man by the name of William Swanson. I used to see Swanson around the Defender studio, but I wasn't sure if he were a part owner. Their company was called the Rex Film Company and for a trademark they used a jeweled crown. One historian notes that the Rex company took over the old Actaphone studio, a little hole in the wall on Eleventh Avenue and 53rd Street owned by Mark Dintenfass, but that is not the case. The Rex company started in a loft building on the west side of Eleventh Avenue between 43rd and 44th Streets. The studio had been enlarged from the one Porter had been using to carry on some talking picture experiments. He had a couple of men working there doing machine work, and, since it was only three blocks from the Defender studio, it was most convenient for him. The Rex company used an old studio that belonged to the Cameraphone company, an early talking picture outfit. Incidentally, Dintenfass was the first person to build a studio in Coytesville or Fort Lee, New Jersey. The year was 1909. Some friends of mine who still live in Coytesville tell me that the building, although somewhat changed, is now occupied by Hansford Brown company.

Porter had added arc light equipment to the new Rex studio, which offered a much greater opportunity for better quality photography. The first picture Rex made was called *A Heroine of '76*. It was a dramatic story about an innkeeper's daughter who accidentally learned of a plot to take the life of George Washington while he was staying at her father's inn. The daughter shows Washington to a different room than the one he was supposed to occupy and takes his room herself, with the result that she is badly wounded. Washington learns the identity of the plotters, thereby ensuring a happy ending.

The role of Washington was taken by a rather good actor, Phillips Smalley, who also had a lot to do with directing the picture. I believe at this point in Edwin S. Porter's career, he began to realize that directing was a full-time job, and concentrated on it more than ever before. Nevertheless, it was a struggle for him to stay away from the camera. He, like Fred Balshofer when he first started out, found it necessary to be able to perform all the duties that went into making a moving picture, including the developing and printing of the film. However, the day of specialization had arrived, and, of course, D. W. Griffith was the great example in the directing field as was Billy Bitzer as a cameraman.

There were others, but not as plentiful as one would think. Biograph and Imp were the companies that created a good number of directors who usually came out of the ranks of the actors. Of the cameramen, some had graduated from the laboratory, while others broke in by working with another cameraman, and naturally still others were relatives. Men with full knowledge of the business were rare, and such men as Porter and Balshofer were destined to become directors or general managers and producers of pictures. It would be hard to say how many craftsmen the two trained, but I am sure the number is great.

In *A Heroine of '76*, a beautiful young actress, Lois Weber, played the innkeeper's daughter, the leading feminine role. In 1927, sixteen years later, I had the pleasure of photographing a picture directed by Miss Weber called *The Angel of Broadway*, starring Leatrice Joy and produced by Cecil B. DeMille at his studio in Culver City. Porter's *A Heroine of '76* was a successful picture and gave me much more experience with a camera. It was Porter's wish that the picture be released on Washington's birthday in 1911, but I don't recall if his wish came true.

At the beginning of 1909 there were about five small independent companies but, instead of all the independents going out of business, the number had increased to over fifteen. To make it more difficult, the territory for the Edison men to police was spreading out. Fred Balshofer had taken his small company to California to make the Bison pictures, the Imp company had gone to Cuba, Powers to Arizona, and the Nestor (Centaur) to Florida. The Imp and Powers companies came back to New York in a few months; Nestor returned for a short stay and then moved to California.

After being chased and hounded by the Patents Company while with Fred Balshofer and the Bison company, the lack of harassment came as a surprise when I worked for Porter and Engel at the Defender and later when Swanson joined them to form the Rex company. The reason for this might have been caused by the change in the independent field. One big factor was that the few independents who had skipped out of reach of the Patents Company had been more than replaced by the rapid growth of the new independent companies and this made the job of policing more difficult. This was the beginning of trying times for the Patents Company in their efforts to enforce their monopoly, and it began to look as if they were faced with an almost impossible task. Whatever the reason, the Rex continued to make their exteriors on Staten Island without the slightest interference.

To illustrate how fast the number of independent companies increased from the beginning of 1909 when the Patents Company was organized until the end of 1912, almost three years later, trademarks of some of these companies are shown on the endpapers. I am sure there were many I haven't recorded.

One important independent was the World, with a studio in Portland, Oregon. This company is not to be confused with the World Film Company that was established later in Fort Lee, New Jersey. One exception shown on the page of trademarks is the Keystone Film Company, included only because their trademark became such an important one. Actually, their trademark didn't come into existence until 1912 when the company was formed as a subsidiary of the New York Motion Picture Company.

For the two years that I worked for Ed Porter, I was learning. This was true, too, for the time I was with Fred Balshofer, for both Porter and Balshofer constantly improved on routine methods of working. The day never finished until the negative shot that day had been developed. Balshofer and Porter were perfectionists and tireless workers. They lived and breathed motion pictures from morning till night.

Porter didn't choose to specialize in any one branch of moving picture making, be it director, cameraman, or producer. He felt he had to be involved in every part of it. I recall one picture we made at the Rex studio. We were photographing a garden scene, a fieldstone wall crossed the set in the background and a painted drop served as the sky. In the foreground there was a small pond of water constructed from a tarred tray about four inches deep. I set a special light to backlight the water, but it would not pick up unless the water had a ripple on the surface. Porter didn't like the way the young fellow outside the camera line was doing the job, so he took over himself and paddled the water with a stick while the actors played the scene. Sometimes he would miss the most important part in order to make sure that some minor effect was done correctly.

In 1919, while shooting an Elsie Ferguson picture that Hugh Ford was directing, Ford, knowing that I had worked for Porter, remarked that Porter could have been at the top of whatever branch of making motion pictures he chose if he had concentrated on that branch alone. Ford had helped direct Pauline Frederick in Rome in 1914 in *The Eternal City*, the last motion picture Porter made. For Edwin S. Porter sticking to one phase of moving pictures was impossible. His inventive urge finally took him out of the production end of motion pictures and brought him into the business of manufacturing Simplex motion picture projectors. The man who began moving pictures as entertainment for the masses abandoned everything he had done to those who followed him.

I began hearing rumors that the Rex was going out of business and that Porter and Engel planned to start a new company. Porter was not the type of man who could be questioned freely, so I went to Joe Engel to find out if there was any truth in what I heard. Engel said, "Yes," and added that he and Porter had already formed a company named Engadine Amusement Company and that they planned to buy pictures produced in Europe, make prints in the Rex laboratory, and sell them to the independent market as George Kleine was doing for the trust.

By the end of 1911, the independents were exhibiting open defiance throughout the industry. The Imp, headed by Carl Laemmle, and the Yankee company with William Steiner at the head, seemed again to be in the midst of the fight. Once before, Bill Steiner and his partner, Bill Paley, a former cameraman, together with the late John Arnold, a cameraman at Yankee at the time, had tried to produce satisfactory pictures using a specially built camera called a Bianchi that did not infringe on the Edison patents. It didn't infringe but neither did it produce a satisfactory picture. Like the rest of the experimental cameras, the picture it produced jumped all over the screen.

Herman Obrock from the Crescent Film days had been quite successful working for the Gaumont company making special short subjects and had decided to go into business for himself in the same field, selling to the exchanges. He had equipped a laboratory in a loft building on Sand Street in Brooklyn. I talked with him at length about the Rex closing and was naturally thinking about another job. He made me an offer to handle the laboratory work of the subjects he shot, which sounded all right to me. At least it was something to do, so I accepted it. When I told Joe Engel I was leaving, he said he thought that Mr. Porter was planning to take me with him when his new company started making pictures at the Crystal studio in New York. This was a different story since previously Engel had said they were going to buy pictures that were made in Europe. He didn't say when Porter was going to start working at the Crystal studio, so I told him there was nothing I could do as I had promised Obrock to start the next day. Engel said he thought I should have told him before taking a job with someone else, and he was right. Later I found out that Porter had joined in partnership with Adolph Zukor and Daniel Frohman to form the Famous Players Company and were making their pictures at the Crystal studio. I realized my impatience caused me to lose out on something that would have afforded me many opportunities.

My new job with Obrock was a pretty lonesome one, as I was alone all day in the laboratory. As in my other jobs, we developed the negatives that Obrock shot each day the same evening, which made some of the working days very long. Being alone in the laboratory all day gave me a lot of time to think about what might have happened if I had not been so impatient but had stayed with Mr. Porter. The letters I got from Fred Balshofer from California were always encouraging and were about my only source of hope.

Chapter 6

FILMING IN THE WILD WEST

FTER A LONG WEARY RIDE of four nights and five days our small company, consisting of Evelyn Graham, Charles French and his wife, Charles Inslee, J. Barney Sherry, Young Deer and his wife Red Wing, Bill Edwards (the prop man), Maxwell Smith, who came in Arthur Miller's place, and I, arrived in Los Angeles the day after Thanksgiving, November, 1909.

We were among the first of the moving picture companies to begin building a moving picture center in California. Los Angeles at that time was a sprawling city of approximately 250,000 residents, many of whom were Spanish-speaking. Their customs and gentle way of life immediately won my admiration and friendship.

In 1909, there was darn little paper money to be had. It was so scarce, in fact, that when I went to the Security Bank on Spring Street, in the heart of the city, and deposited two thousand dollars in twenty, fifty, and one hundred-dollar bills to the account of the New York Motion Picture Company, the clerks eyed me as though I had held up a train. When I asked the teller to change a twenty-dollar bill for ones, he handed me "cartwheels." "Bills," I said. He shook his head but managed to find five one-dollar bills, and I was obliged to take the remainder in silver dollars.

Just about the first to come to California to make movies, I believe, was Colonel William (Bill) Selig, who sent Francis

The Bison Company in 1910. The original company that came from New York to California in 1909. Those italicized came from New York. 1. *Charles French*, 2. Charles Avery, 3. Frank Montgomery, 4. *Evelyn Graham*, 5. *Maxwell Smith*, 6. Tex Cooper, 7. Jewell Darrel, 8. T. K. Peters, 9. Major McGuire, 10. *Red Wing*, 11. *J. Barney Sherry*, 12. *William Gibbons*, 13. Marguerite Favar, 14. Jess McGaugh, 15. *Young Deer*, 16. *Fred Balshofer*, 17. Milt Brown. Published courtesy of T.K. Peters Library, Austin Texas.

Boggs, his ace director, and a few actors to Los Angeles in the fall of 1907 to establish a studio of sorts in a former Chinese laundry on Olive Street not far from the center of the city. In January, 1910, the Biograph company sent a unit headed by D. W. Griffith with Mary Pickford, Henry B. Walthall, and Billy Bitzer, to name a few, out to Los Angeles. They established a studio in a vacant carbarn at Georgia and Pico streets, on the southwest side of the city. Gilbert M. Anderson (real name Aaronson), a six-foot rugged individual of about thirty-five, who made the character of Broncho Billy famous, was George K. Spoor's partner in the Essanay Film Manufacturing Company and was making western pictures starring himself in Niles, California, nearly four hundred and fifty miles north of Los Angeles.

Like the Biograph, we intended to return to New York in

the spring, so we set up a temporary studio in a former grocery and feed store that had a large barn and some old shacks on a fenced-in plot of ground on Alessandro Street, which was a hilly, sparsely settled section some three miles west of Los Angeles. We converted the store and shacks into dressing rooms for our players and put up a small outdoor stage where we could shoot our interiors. The rented property included a small house across the street that I used as an office and as a place to lock up the camera equipment. There also was enough space for a small laboratory to develop the daily negatives, which I had to do myself until I trained a former cook from the Alexandria Hotel.

I would cut the negative scene by scene, leaving about six inches extra at each end, and number them, starting with scene one, two, and so on; the main, sub-, and spoken titles I wrote and sent with the developed picture negative to be photographed in our laboratory in Brooklyn. In those days, the negative of a complete reel or picture was not joined in one roll for printing; certain scenes were selected to be toned or tinted different colors, so these scenes had to be printed in separate rolls and handled on separate drums. The girls who assembled the positive prints worked at a bench on which there was a row of numbered wooden pegs. The joiners, as they were called, cut the individual scenes from each roll, and the number of a particular scene was placed on the corresponding numbered peg. On the rewinder a piece of the leader was put first, then the main and subtitle, followed by scene one, two, and so on, including the descriptive and spoken titles. The finished reel or picture had a splice at the beginning and end of each scene and title. As there were no machines or even guides to make splices, the accuracy of the splice depended upon the skill of the joiner. The above seems fantastic compared with modern film processing. Today the full reel of a picture has hardly a splice.

Col. William Selig had come to Los Angeles to avoid the wintry blasts of Chicago and had intended to return in the spring. Instead, he decided to stay. Selig was a short, heavyset man about forty who had been a traveling salesman and magician before he organized his moving picture company in Chicago in 1897. Judging by the looks of his new studio in California it was obvious that he was making money hand over fist. His studio in Edendale covered a city block on Alessandro Street and was half a block or more wide, surrounded by a high, vine-clad wall. Huge wrought-iron gates of Spanish design formed the entrance to the studio, and just beyond the gates was a lush tropical garden.

It was here that such coming stars as Tom Santschi, Hobart Bosworth, William Farnum, and Robert Leonard, among others, played in his pictures. Late in the summer of 1910 Francis Boggs, top director for Selig, was shot to death in the studio garden by a Japanese gardener who went berserk. When Selig attempted to take the gun away from the gardener, he was shot in the arm. Selig might have been fatally wounded had not others arrived in time to overpower the gun-brandishing Japanese, who, for no apparent reason, was all for killing Selig too.

As far as I know, there is no actual record of who was the first to photograph a movie scene in Hollywood. Dave Horsley has the distinction of being the first person to establish a studio when he took over a former tavern on the corner of Sunset Boulevard and Gower Street in the fall of 1911. As early as January, 1910, however, we photographed scenes around Hollywood, riding our horses from the studio in Edendale to the picturesque hills over the winding roads. There were some adobe buildings on a fair-sized ranch just west of LaBrea Avenue and Hollywood Boulevard where we photographed many horse chases, gun battles, stagecoach holdups and other similar scenes for our Bison pictures before we discovered Griffith Park. Griffith Park was a beautiful place with tree-covered hills, ideal for western pictures. It was only a few miles from our studio, and many times we set up an Indian village and left it there for days at a time in the section now known as Griffith Park golf course.

We were doing fine in California and hadn't yet see McCoy or any of his henchmen so we decided to stay. We began to convert our temporary studio into a permanent one. Our stock

company of actors and actresses had grown to include Jewell
Darrell, Marguerite Favar, Marin (named for Marin County
where she was born) Sais, George Gebhardt, Art Acord, Jack
Conway, Art Ortega, Roy Purden, Frank Montgomery, Howard
Davies, Princess Mona Darkfeather, Ann (Anna) Little, Jess
McGaugh, Tex Cooper, Charlie Avery and several others. We
also had Bebe Daniels, a child actress, and her mother, Phyllis,
who acted as my secretary and bookkeeper.

I had bought several horses to use in our western pictures,
some of them from a Mexican fellow. The day he delivered
them he was mounted on the most magnificent white stallion
I had ever seen. The minute I saw that horse all I could think
of was what a valuable addition it would be to our Bison
pictures. I tried every argument I could think of to convince the
Mexican to sell us the horse, but he simply wouldn't listen.
However, I was able to make a deal to rent the horse for one
picture. We had just started the film and were shooting some
scenes at the old wooden bridge that used to be on Los Feliz
Road near the entrance to Griffith Park when Jack Conway
came thundering across the bridge on the white stallion. A
plank loosened and the edge struck the horse a severe blow
across his forelegs causing him to fall. Conway was sent
sprawling but fortunately was not hurt. One of the cowboys
ran to put his weight on the horse's head to prevent him from
getting up, while others did what they could to quiet the
animal. It appeared as though he had broken his leg.

Jess McGaugh, who was in charge of our horses, took over
and did a fine job on the foreleg which turned out to be
severely lacerated but not broken. The Mexican owner became quite excited over the incident. He had no idea what the
injury amounted to and could well wonder about the soundness
of the horse after taking such a spill, even if the stallion hadn't
suffered a broken leg. McGaugh estimated the veterinary
charges at seventy-five dollars, and if the Mexican insisted on
being paid for rental of the horse during the time it was out
of action, it seemed better to buy the horse at it was. McGaugh
thought that the owner, under the present circumstances, might
be willing to sell, so I talked it over with him. The result was

that I bought the beautiful white stallion for a hundred dollars
on the strength of McGaugh's opinion that he would be as
good as new in a month or so.

What a bargain this proved to be! While the horse was
healing, I made plans to feature him in one of our Bison pictures. I chose the obvious name of Snowball for him as he was
snow white without a mark on him. In his first picture, I took
advantage of every opportunity to insert his name in the
spoken titles. When the picture was shipped east and my
partners saw it, they wired me to "Buy that horse called Snowball even if you have to pay a thousand dollars." It delighted
me to be able to wire back, "We own Snowball. Bought him
for $100." Snowball became well known to movie audiences
throughout the country; bags of mail were received asking for
more pictures with Snowball in them. With our famous horse
and Inslee in his naked Indian hero roles, our Bison pictures
were outselling most of the pictures made by members of the
trust. This was a bitter pill for them to swallow.

Not long after that, Kessel and Bauman, who had been
visiting in California for a few weeks and were about ready
to go back East, and I were sitting in the lobby of the Alexandria Hotel in Los Angeles enjoying an after-dinner smoke.
I noticed a man sitting across from us. What drew my attention
to him was that he was holding the newspaper he was pre-
tending to read upside down. The top of his head, which
was all that showed above the newspaper, looked familiar. I

Fred Balshofer
mounted on Snowball.

kept watching him, and sure enough, it was the old snooper himself, Al McCoy, the Patents Company detective. I nudged Kessel, pointed and whispered, "Al McCoy." Kessel studied him awhile and told me I was imagining things. He insisted and said, "I'll bet you a five-dollar gold piece that's not McCoy." I replied, "I'll take your bet." Kessel smiled and wanted to know how I could prove it. I said I'd go over and talk to him. I stood up and walked over to where the man was sitting and stood looking down at him. "Hello, Slim," I said, smiling. "What are you doing way out here?" I honestly felt sorry for McCoy at that moment. He looked up at me like the cat that swallowed the canary. "It's my job, Fred," he said in an apologetic manner. Calling me Fred sounded like he wanted to be on a sort of friendly basis. "I'd hate to see you get hurt," I answered in a pleasant tone, "but you're out West now and the cowboys here are a real tough bunch. They carry six-shooters, and I don't think they want to be interfered with." I really put it on and could see that it was having an effect. I continued, "I'm giving you a friendly tip. Don't start anything here or you're going to run into trouble. I'll keep quiet about your being here and the rest is up to you." With that I left him, walked back to Addie Kessel, and collected the five-dollar gold piece. I didn't think we would have any trouble with McCoy and told Kessel and Bauman they could leave as planned and not to worry.

McCoy took my advice and kept himself pretty scarce, but every now and then I would see him standing on a rise watching us through field glasses. I never told anyone who he was, as some of the scare talk I had handed him at the hotel wasn't without basis. Whenever I spotted him, I'd send one of the cowboys riding in his direction with instructions just to inquire who he was, but McCoy always disappeared before the rider reached him. A couple of weeks went by without my seeing him so I thought he had become discouraged and departed. This proved to be a poor guess. It wasn't long before I learned I had made a mistake.

One Saturday night I went up to visit George Gebhardt, who lived on the hill overlooking our studio in Edendale. During the course of the evening, his wife, Madeline, went to the back porch to get something and noticed a light in my office. She thought it was unusual at that hour so she told me about it. Gebhardt got out his forty-five gun, and he and I started down the hill to investigate. We arrived at the office just as the lights went out. It was mighty dark on the porch, but Gebhardt had his gun ready for anything that might happen. In spite of the dark, we could make out the figure of a man tiptoeing his way out the side door. Gebhardt jammed the gun in the man's back and barked "Hands up." A package dropped to the porch floor with a thump as he made haste to comply. "Don't shoot," he cried. "It's me." You could have knocked me over with the proverbial feather when I discovered it was Maxwell Smith, my camera boy and the only other person I trusted with a key to the place. He blabbered out a confession that he had made sketches and used the office lights and our 5x7 still camera in an effort to make photographs for McCoy of the inside movement of my Pathé movie camera. I found the plate holders where he had dropped them on the porch floor and smashed them. Smith nearly had succeeded in his plan but almost lost his life for a few measly dollars. As a matter of fact, he did lose his life from a shotgun blast a short time later while on a hunting trip with his uncle who accidentally shot him in the stomach.

This incident with Smith made me more cautious than ever, and I never left the camera in the office after that. I took it home with me every evening and brought it back the next morning. Weekends and between pictures, I wrapped the Pathé in a Navajo blanket and stored it in a large safety box I had rented for the purpose in the Commercial Bank in downtown Los Angeles, where we had our bank account. Although I hadn't seen hide nor hair of McCoy since I fired Smith, I often wondered what his next move would be.

Late in 1910 Charlie French made other connections, which meant that I had to take over the entire directing job. It was impossible to get any kind of a cameraman in Los Angeles then, so I had to operate the camera as well as direct our pictures for the next several months. Then I broke in Robert Newhard, a hard-working youth I had hired after the Smith fiasco.

To add to my troubles, I was subpoenaed by the Patents

Company to be examined at a deposition hearing in Los Angeles, as they were preparing an infringement suit against us in New York. Kessel and Bauman came out to California post-haste when I wired them the bad news. When they arrived, they too, were subpoenaed to be examined. Our patent attorneys, Lyon and Lyon, together with our regular attorney, Frank Graham, got them out of appearing by pleading that Kessel and Bauman were nonresidents. On the advice of all our lawyers, they went back to New York, leaving me to face the situation alone. The attorneys for the Patents Company knew their subject well, and it wasn't very long before they had me hanging by a thin thread with their questions as to what kind of a camera I was using.

"What make is it? Describe it. Can you make a sketch of it, and the movement?" I shook my head. "I don't know how to draw," I said, and then gave them a run-around story by describing another French camera that I well remembered and that was not an infringement of the Edison patents. They were well aware that I was telling them a fish story, but they had to prove it. They brought up the fact that I had rented a safety deposit box at the Commercial Bank, which I had to admit. How the lawyers found this out I don't know, but I began to sweat. Luckily, lunch recess was called moments later. "What about that safety deposit box? Is the camera in it?", Graham asked when he and I were alone on our way to lunch. When I nodded "Yes," he told me the opposing attorneys would seek a court order to examine it. I had no time for lunch; the most important thing was to get the camera out of the safety deposit box immediately.

Buster Edmonds, one of our actors who also drove for me sometimes, was sitting behind the wheel of my car where he had parked when he drove me down to the hearing. He was the only other person who knew about the camera being in the safety deposit box. Or was he? I was in a spot, and I put the question to him. Edmonds swore he had never told anyone, not even his wife, about it. We rushed over to the bank. Edmonds stayed in the car while I hurried in, took the camera out of the box, and made sure that the Navajo blanket covered it completely before I passed the vault clerk. I hustled out of the bank, put the camera in the car with Edmonds, and told him to get going. "Take it home and keep it until I want it again, but above all keep mum," were my instructions.

Sure enough, the Patents Company's attorneys obtained a court order to examine the safety deposit box, and, headed by a deputy sheriff, we all marched over to the bank where I was identified by the vault clerk. I then led them to the safety deposit box where I produced my key. Lyon and Lyon didn't know what to expect and looked grave, as did Graham, while the opposing attorneys were quite cocky. So sure of themselves were they, in fact, that when the box was opened and found to be empty they just stood there and gaped in utter disbelief. Graham grinned with satisfaction and shrugged his shoulders, and that was that.

I had no idea what was in the wind nor what the Patents Company's next move would be. I thought back to the time when we sneaked out of Coytesville up to Neversink, New York and lost their detectives. That maneuver had enabled us to work nearly all summer without being bothered. If it worked then, why not try it now? I hustled all of us up to Big Bear Valley, a remote and practically unknown summer resort in the heart of the San Bernardino mountains, which was some ninety

Red Wing and Young Deer in *Little Dove's Romance*, one of the pictures made by Balshofer in Big Bear Valley in 1911 while the Bison company was hiding from the Patents Company detectives.

miles east of Los Angeles with twenty-five miles of tough, steep grades no auto could navigate. Those twenty-five miles meant travel on horseback and buckboard from San Bernardino, a small town in the shadow of the mountain range.

The members of the company that made the long trek were Charles Inslee, Princess Mona Darkfeather, Jack Conway, Hoot Gibson, Art Acord, J. Barney Sherry, Frank Montgomery, Art Ortega, Eugene Allen, George Gebhardt and his wife, Steve Barton and his wife, and Roy Purden. Ann Little came up later to replace Mona Darkfeather as our leading lady when Mona, along with Frank Montgomery, left to take other jobs.

In those early days Big Bear Valley was really wild country. The less rugged but much longer road up the mountain was by way of Victorville, on the Mojave·Desert side. Over this road, well in advance of the company, we sent our horse-drawn wagons loaded with heavy equipment. One wagon carried five or six canoes which we later camouflaged with bark taken from the plentiful mountainside aspen trees. When finished, the canoes bore a surprisingly close resemblance to real Indian birchbark canoes.

The shorter road up the south side of the mountain was by way of Clark's Canyon Road which took from sunrise to sunset to climb. It wound around boulders and along narrow footpaths that had been reinforced on the edge. There were deep canyons below. At places, surefooted animals were needed to navigate with a fair amount of safety. If there were no delays, it was possible to reach the appropriately named Clark's Halfway House just about midday. Lunch was served at this welcome resting place, and here the animals rested and were watered and fed before making the climb to the top of the mountain.

We were the first to make moving pictures at Big Bear Valley, but I must confess that the Patents Company forced this distinction upon us. Big Bear Lake is a large body of water, surrounded by giant fir trees, picturesque meadows edged with huge boulders, and in nearly every direction were vistas of snowcapped mountains that afforded beautiful backgrounds. Our Indians paddling along the lakeshore from one village to

Little Dove's Gratitude made at Big Bear, California, in 1911.

another provided atmosphere and color such as had never been seen before in western pictures. All this increased the popularity of Bison pictures.

Any required location was never more than half a mile from our living quarters, an establishment built by a fellow who lived in San Bernardino as an accommodation for hunters during the duck-hunting season. We rented the entire outfit, consisting of several rustic, weather-beaten log cabins, each of which took care of two persons. The cabins were equipped with stone fireplaces and plenty of cord wood was stacked outside. I used one of the cabins as an office and living quarters, and a few of the others were occupied by the married couples in the company.

There also was a central building, called the Round House, which had a balcony that went completely around the interior. The balcony was about twelve feet from the floor and provided access to bedrooms. In the center of the large lounge and recreation room was a fire pit where we burned logs on cool evenings. On one side was the entrance hall to the dining hall.

With the exception of Inslee, the company cooperated in every way and seemed to be having a fine time. I managed to knock out one picture after another without any trouble, even though we often were bothered by thousands of wild ducks that made the lake their home. Many times when we played a scene that required the firing of guns, the ducks would rise from the lake so closely bunched as to have the same effect as a cloud covering the sun, and we would have to retake the scene. It didn't take us long to realize that a simple remedy for this was to fire a shot in the air, then quickly photograph a scene before the ducks could collect on the lake again. We never learned how to cope with the gray squirrels that made a habit of dropping out of the trees when we were photographing. Sometimes they landed on the ground so close to an actor as to startle him and spoil the scene.

Each weekend our exposed negative was turned over to a cowboy who took it down the mountain and then expressed it by train to Los Angeles, where it was picked up and delivered to the laboratory at Edendale to be developed. The developed negatives from the previous week's work was returned to Big Bear Valley in the same fashion. Sundays and evenings were utilized for cutting the negatives and marking each scene and writing titles, as previously described. Then the negative was ready to be shipped to New York. Fortunately for us, McCoy, who was hanging around the Edendale studio trying to find out where we had gone, never learned the secret of this procedure or our location.

For the actors, Sunday was a day of recreation. Those so inclined spent the day catching pink salmon trout from the teeming lake. That night all of us enjoyed a wonderful trout dinner at the Round House. Others of the company spent the day writing stories. I paid ten dollars for those used; Acord, Gebhardt, and Inslee collected most of the money.

When our laboratory in South Brooklyn could no longer take care of the volume of positive prints required to supply the demand for Bison brand pictures, we built the most modern laboratory of those times on West Nineteenth Street in New York City, on the second floor of an eight- or ten-story office building. The laboratory was equipped with the new Bell & Howell continuous printers and precision perforators. The "wet" side of the lab had the latest in rack and tank systems. Doc Willat, an expert in his line, was in charge.

The three partners, Kessel, Bauman and I, were declaring dividends amounting to about twelve hundred to thirteen hundred dollars a week in addition to drawing salaries, with no income tax to pay. Work and responsibility were also mounting even though Robert Newhard, with a little help, was about ready to take full charge as the cameraman. Nevertheless, directing, preparing the next story for shooting, plus the full responsibility for the company became more than any one individual could find time to handle properly. Early in August I wrote to my partners in New York to tell them that the work had increased to the point where I could no longer handle it alone. I suggested that they send out a director and a cameraman to help carry some of the load. Originally I had planned to give Charlie Inslee a chance at directing, but it became increasingly clear that he could not measure up to the task. In my letter to my partners I mentioned the Biograph or Imp companies as possible sources for these men since those two seemed to be the producers that were developing talent in these fields. I mentioned George Loane Tucker or Herbert Brenon of Imp as possible directors but left it up to my partners to choose a cameraman.

Chapter 7

WITH THE PATHÉ NEWS WEEKLY

ERMAN OBROCK'S ENTERPRISE of making short films and
running a commercial laboratory was not successful during
a little over a year of existence. The demand for short
subjects, unless they were of national importance, had become
less and less, largely because Gaumont and Pathé weeklies
had their own cameramen covering all sections of the country.
The small amount of laboratory work for the few that were
shooting short subjects was of no consequence as far as de-
fraying the expenses of running the laboratory.

In February, 1913, Obrock had photographed a subject covering the launching of a battleship at the Brooklyn Navy
Yard close to our laboratory on Sand Street. We developed the
negative and made a rush print. The next day I took the print
over to the Pathé News Weekly offices at 1 Congress Street,
Jersey City Heights, with the idea of selling the subject to
their news department. Mr. Leo Franconie, the man I had come
to see, was anxious to look at what I had and handed the film
to the operator. He and I went into the projection room, and
when the film was finished, Franconie said he could use it.

As we came out of the projection room, I was delighted to
bump into my old friend Al Richard from New York Motion
Picture Company days. While Mr. Franconie went into his
office to arrange for a check for the film he had bought, Richard
and I started talking. I told him of Obrock's predicament and
added that my job there couldn't last much longer. Richard
asked me if I'd like a job on the Pathé News Weekly. I cer-

tainly appreciated his kindness, but I had my doubts as to my qualifications for I had had no experience whatsoever in the news field. Al gave me the old line that everybody had to start some time, and before I really made up my mind he ushered me into Mr. Franconie's office. Al gave Franconie a long pitch about what a great cameraman I was, but I insisted on telling him that I never had done any news work. My lack of experience in the news field didn't seem to bother Franconie in the slightest. He suggested that if I were interested he would have another news cameraman work with me to teach me the ropes.

All the way back to the lab in Brooklyn I kept thinking that Al Richard had oversold me, and I was worried about getting into something that I couldn't handle. At the laboratory, I explained the situation to Obrock. To my surprise he seemed relieved as well as pleased with the prospects of my getting another job. He had been thinking of closing the laboratory anyway, he said, and he encouraged me to take the offer, telling me I would make a good news cameraman. The next day I went out to the Pathé studio and was hired by Mr. Franconie, who made arrangements to send me on the road with an experienced news cameraman named Joe Rucker. I was fortunate, for Rucker was not only able to teach me but also he was willing.

The news cameraman's job in those days was very different from what it is today. There was no sound and everything had to be conveyed visually with as much continuity as possible. The restriction on the amount of film one subject could stand made full coverage of some a little difficult. Long, descriptive titles interpreting the subject were undesirable. Today's television news has the advantage of someone explaining to the viewer what he is looking at from start to finish.

Joe and I made our headquarters at the Ansonia Hotel in Detroit, but we covered a territory of about three hundred miles in all directions. Each day we bought out-of-town as well as local newspapers, scanned them for likely subjects, present and upcoming. We were always able to make arrangements for sports subjects in advance. The Pathé News Weekly card acted like a magic wand in those days. Everybody welcomed the Weekly cameraman. Sometimes it was necessary to fake the photographing of some of the dignitaries who showed up and insisted on getting into the act. We tricked them easily by fixing the crank so it turned without operating the shaft of the camera and therefore no film went through. All in all, it was an exciting and interesting job, one where the cameraman was entirely responsible for the product, and the spirit of friendly competition among the other news cameramen offered a constant challenge.

There was no bulky equipment to haul around — just the camera, tripod, and a few rolls of extra film. The camera we used was called the Pathé news model, which was lightweight, and the back, sides, and top raised from the back forward, providing access to the round, metal magazines which held four hundred feet of negative film. The camera crank was on the right-hand side, and the focus device at the back. This made it possible to change focus simply by glancing from the upside-down image on the ground glass of the finder on the left-hand side to the focusing scale at the back. The camera's only fault was that it produced quite a lot of static in cold weather. After Rucker was sent out on another assignment and I was left on my own, Detroit remained my base of operation. There were all kinds of winter and summer sports on Lake St. Clair, around Bell Isle and Grosse Point. Ice boat racing is a really exciting sport and made an excellent news subject.

The office had sent me a studio model Pathé camera in the hope that it would not create as much static as the news model. Static, for the benefit of those who may not be familiar with the term as applied to motion picture making, was produced in the camera by friction of the celluloid side of the film as it slid by the steel pressure plate at the aperture as well as the velvet at the light traps of the magazines. The blue static sparks exposed the negative causing the developed negative to be full of black marks resembling branches of a Christmas tree. When the weather turned cold, static was the bugaboo of all cameramen. Some time later Eastman Kodak came up with a remedy for static by coating the celluloid side of the film with a thin gum substance that prevented friction. This

Arthur Miller in 1912
at work for the Pathé Weekly.
The bulge on the cloth
covering the magazines
was caused by hot water bottles
held snugly against the magazines
to prevent static.

practically solved the problem of static. Looking at a piece of negative film today, it is not possible to tell that it has been static-proofed, as the gum coating has long since been replaced by a coating that is undetectable. Static now is almost non-existent.

Each cameraman had his own idea how to cure the situation. Some drove an iron stake into the frozen ground to which they attached a piece of copper wire. This reached to the metal part of the inside of the camera. It was thought that any static electricity generated would thus be carried off by the copper ground wire. One photographer, I recall, placed an uncorked bottle of ammonia inside his camera and claimed that the fumes from it prevented static. Whether they did or not, I never knew. Billy Bitzer had a hole made in the side of his Pathé studio model camera. Below it he attached a carbide lamp of the kind the youngsters used on their bicycles in that era. From the top of the lamp was a tube to convey the heat. from the lighted lamp into the camera. Others left camera and film out in the cold all the time on the theory that if both were the same temperature there would be no static. In the frantic efforts to prevent static on film, some of the gadgets and beliefs bordered on voodooism. Certainly there was no scientific knowledge behind the experiments, and many cameramen were hired simply because of their reputation for producing films without static. It must be added that many cameramen owned their own cameras.

It seemed to me, at the time, that the most practical method for avoiding static was to have a felt pad made with pockets on each side that were large enough to hold a rubber hot water bottle. The pad was laid across the two magazines at the top of the camera, holding a hot water bottle at each side of the magazine. Slipped over this was a fitted cloth sack that held the bottles tight against the magazines and also helped to retain heat. When the camera was not in actual use, I covered it with a heavy horse blanket. In this manner I photographed the finals of the ice boat races at Grosse Point when the temperature was not much above zero. The water was replenished in the rubber bottle at least twice that day. When the negative had been shipped to the home office, a wire arrived saying that it was exciting and that there was no static, which made me very happy.

When I read in January or February in a Buffalo newspaper that a rare event was taking place at Niagara Falls because of the extreme cold, I hurried over to make a news film. Part of the Falls had frozen over and presented an unusual and fantastic sight that attracted thousands of sightseers. The newspapers hadn't exaggerated in the slightest the beauty of this winter wonderland. After photographing the Falls from what I considered to be the most advantageous angles, I went back to Detroit and had already shipped the film to New York when it dawned on me that I had invaded another cameraman's territory. But since I had gone to the Canadian side of the Falls to do the photographing, I hoped there wouldn't be too much of a howl. Instead, Franconie wired me praising the picture for its beauty and lack of static. He also suggested that I try for news pictures involving people and perhaps occasionally do one of the arty type.

About the first of April, 1914, I received a wire ordering me to return to the home office with all of my equipment. I had no idea why I should be called back as I now had begun to know a little something about my assigned territory. When

I arrived in the office I went directly to Franconie's office. He seemed to be waiting for me and said the head man of the studio, Louis Gasnier, wanted to see me upstairs in the studio. He said that Gasnier had seen the film I made at Niagara Falls and wanted to talk to me. Louis Gasnier was the head of the Pathé studio, in charge of theatrical production, but had nothing to do with the News Weekly part of the operation. Gasnier greeted me with a handshake, but I had trouble understanding him as his English had a strong French accent. After he told me he had seen the subject I photographed at Niagara Falls and was impressed by it, he surprised me by saying he had talked with Al Richard who told him of my studio production experience. We discussed my initial training by Fred Balshofer and then with Edwin S. Porter.

While I went on with my story, I could see Mr. Gasnier had something on his mind. He began by saying he had started to make a picture in St. Augustine, Florida, but was not satisfied with the cameraman he had taken down there and thought I could do the job instead. Gasnier's original idea was to take a Frenchman by the name of Avar as his cameraman. Avar was the head of the camera shop; the idea was that if anything went wrong with the camera, Avar could readily repair it. It soon became apparent, however, that while Avar might be an excellent camera repairman, he certainly was not a very good cameraman. Their reasoning seems pretty fantastic today. Gasnier told me that Avar was now back working in the machine shop repairing cameras.

From Gasnier's talk, I gathered that they had finished half of the first episode of a serial they intended to make. At this juncture, he sent me downstairs to tell Mr. Franconie that I was no longer in the news department but would be working upstairs in the studio. Louis Gasnier also informed me that my next assignment was to photograph their new serial, with Harry Wood as my second cameraman. Early in April, 1914, I started shooting the first episode of a serial that became well known as *The Perils of Pauline*.

Chapter 8

THE KEYSTONE FILM COMPANY AND
RIVALRY AMONG THE COMPANIES

I KNEW THAT when the weather turned cold we would be forced to leave Big Bear Valley and return to the Edendale studio in Los Angeles, where once again our troubles would start with the Patents Company and their detectives. In anticipation of that problem, I planned to use a large piece of property, some several thousand acres, we had leased from the Santa Monica Water and Power Company some time before we went up to Big Bear Valley. The property was just north of the town of Santa Monica and included Santa Ynez Canyon in the Santa Monica Mountains. The only entrance to Santa Ynez Canyon was from the town of Santa Monica along the beach road that paralleled the Pacific Ocean. We had used this location for making Bison pictures for quite a while and had built a few shacks in the canyon where a couple of cowboys lived and cared for some horses we kept there permanently. My idea was to fence a portion of this property in Santa Ynez Canyon, including some of the surrounding choice locations, and post the fenced area with signs reading "Private Property —Keep Out." Four or five cowboys would ride the fenced boundary on the lookout for snoopers.

Late in the fall of 1911 the cold and threatening snow forced us to leave Big Bear Valley. About this time the Imp Company came to California and established a studio in Boyle Heights

New York Motion Picture stock company in 1911. BOTTOM ROW, *left*: Red Wing, Fred Balshofer, little girl in *center* Bebe Daniels, man holding hat, Charles O. Bauman, and *standing at right*, Young Deer. SECOND ROW: Marin Sais, back of little boy Bebe's mother Phyllis. *Second from right*, Evelyn Graham. THIRD ROW: *extreme left*, Maxwell Smith. *Fifth from left* Jack Conway, later an M. G. M. director. TOP ROW: *Extreme left*, Art Acord; *fourth from left*, Pat Hartigan, and *fifth from left*, J. Barney Sherry.

in East Los Angeles, and Dave Horsley brought his company to Hollywood where he took over an old tavern on the corner of Gower Street and Sunset Boulevard which he converted into a studio.

Bauman, too, came out but only on a visit. He agreed with my idea of fencing in the selected area, and in the course of our conversation, he told me that both the directors I had suggested they hire had wanted too much money so they had employed a young director, Thomas H. Ince, for a hundred and twenty-five dollars a week, as well as Ray Smallwood as cameraman.

Bauman learned that the Miller Brothers 101 Ranch Wild West show was in winter quarters at Venice, California, just a few miles down the coast from our location. Together we went to look over the show and the possibility of using it in our Bison pictures during the time they were wintering there. We talked out a deal with Joe Miller who was in charge of the show. I made out a personal check for a thousand dollars, payable to the Miller Brothers 101 Ranch to bind the deal. Of course, I was later reimbursed by the Company.

Our arrangement gave us the use of about seventy-five cowboys, twenty-five cowgirls, and about thirty-five Indians and their squaws, who spoke no English. One of the tribe, a rather fat squaw who called herself Minnie, was their teacher and interpreter. We hired Jim Brooks, manager of the show, who was a powerful ex-cowpuncher well able to rustle everybody up at sunrise and parade them up the coast to our sanctuary in the Santa Ynez Canyon, to be in charge of them. We also had the use of twenty-four oxen, some bison, and many horses complete with trappings, as well as prairie schooners and stage coaches.

Near the end of October, Ince arrived. He was accompanied by his wife, Ray Smallwood as cameraman, Ethel Grandon as a leading lady, and Charlie Weston. They immediately began making pictures at the Edendale studio.

The year 1912 was a hectic one for us. Some of our Bison pictures were being duped and run in small theaters out in the sticks. I made the return trip to New York with Charlie Bauman as I had an idea of how to build a printer that would expose the words "New York Motion Picture Company, Inc." outside the picture area along the perforations of each film. The printer was simply a brass cylinder the width of 35mm film and about three inches in diameter, with sprocket teeth on one side and the name of the company perforated through the metal on the other. Inside the cylinder was a printing light, the brightness of which could be controlled by the size bulb used as well as the speed the cylinder turned, or a combina-

tion of both. A shaft and flange at one end of the machine held
the roll of positive film, which was fed through the printer by
a motor-driven shaft and sprocket at the other end, where a
take-up flange was provided. As the perforations rode on the
teeth at one side of the printing cylinder, it turned continually,
exposing the name of the company. Consequently, when the
film was developed, as well as the prints, the name of the company ran along the perforations. It was worth the trouble because many of the theater owners we notified refused to accept
prints not having this identification, but it did not stop the
duping operation entirely.

Shortly after the first of the year, while I was in New York,
we formed the Keystone Film Company in New York City, and
hired Mack Sennett, a ruddy-faced, barrel-chested ex-actor
from the Biograph company as director and leading man. Mabel Normand, a trim, five-foot, big-eyed brunette beauty of
seventeen was the leading lady. The principal players were
Ford Sterling, Fred Mace, and Henry "Pathé" Lehrman. In addition to managing the Bison company, it now became my responsibility to manage the newly formed Keystone company.

The first three pictures were made in and around New York
about the middle of February, and they were what we called
split-reelers, which meant that there were two separate comedies on one reel, each comedy being less than five hundred
feet in length. It took us about eight or ten days to shoot the
lot at a cost of approximately fifteen hundred dollars.

We called the first picture we shot *Cohen At Coney Island.*
The reason we chose Coney Island for the background was
that we could make use of a lot of film I had photographed
at Coney Island in 1908 and sold to Kessel and Bauman while
I had the Crescent Film Company. Sennett directed scenes
with the few actors we had, plus a couple of extras. This was
to be matched and sandwiched in with the shots of Coney
Island we already had. It didn't work out as well as we expected; when the picture was finally released months later, it
was called simply *At Coney Island.*

Our second comedy we named *Riley and Schultz,* with Sennett playing Riley and Ford Sterling in the first of the Dutch-

man roles he later made famous. I can't remember the title of the third picture, but I do remember cutting and assembling all three at our new laboratory on West Nineteenth Street. This was the first time I had seen the new lab and I was fascinated by the Bell & Howell continuous printers and their precision-built perforators which punched four holes on each side of the film in one stroke. The difference between the new Bell & Howell perforators and the Eberhard Schneider perforators, which punched one hole on each side of the film and ran at only half the speed, was comparable to that between a Model T Ford and a Rolls Royce.

Doc Willat, who ran our laboratory, mentioned that he had heard the same company now was building a new movie camera. I had plans to visit Miller Brothers 101 Ranch, near Bliss (now Marland), Oklahoma en route to Los Angeles so I called Donald Bell of Bell & Howell on the telephone and made an appointment to stop off at their Chicago plant to look at their new camera.

Their shop was in a walk-up loft building where Donald Bell and his partner, Howell, were busy assembling their new cameras and tripods, one at a time. The price was much higher than the Pathé studio model, the most popular camera at that time, so they didn't seem to be working too hard filling orders. One camera, used for demonstration, was mounted on its tripod, and it had a completely different appearance from any camera I had seen before. I gave the crank a spin. After I let go, the crank made two or three turns before it came to a stop. The camera was constructed entirely on an aluminum alloy with all the shafts turning in ball bearings. Both the feed and take-up magazines were of one casting and, when placed on top by turning a knurled disc, a threaded screw fastened the magazine to the camera. Film fed out of the unexposed side of the magazines and entered the exposed side that fitted into a groove cast in the top of the camera. This made a foolproof light trap and eliminated a weakness of the Pathé camera. The take-up spool in the magazine was driven by a spring belt from a pulley on one of the camera shafts.

The Bell & Howell camera had two revolutionary features,

one of which was termed a "shuttle." When the film was in motion, the tension was released at the aperture and during exposure, the pressure plate tension was applied. The shuttle was easily removed for cleaning. The second, equally revolutionary, feature was the revolving turret with four mounted lenses of different focal lengths. Part of the camera was a spring dovetailed arrangement on the bottom that slid into a matching groove on the tilt head, which actually was the top section on the tripod. By turning a crank, the camera could be panned horizontally. By turning a crank on the tilt, it could be moved up or down vertically.

George K. Spoor of the Essanay company was the first to have one of his cameramen use this new camera. It was rumored that Spoor had financed Bell & Howell when the company started making printers and perforators, but no one seemed to know if this were true. Donald Bell told me who had purchased their second camera, but I can't recall the name. Before I left their office, though, I had purchased the third one for the New York Motion Picture Company. Delivery was promised for some time in the fall. I know for certain that Broncho Billy Anderson, making Essanay westerns in Niles, California, was still using the first model Bell & Howell built. That model was more like all the other cameras in a wooden case, although it had one feature no other camera had. The lens could be raised or lowered, similar to the lens board on a still camera.

Taking the railroad out of Chicago, I continued my trip to Ponca City, Oklahoma. Joe Miller met me at the train and we drove over some rough roads for almost an hour before finally reaching the ranch. The purpose of my visit was to ascertain if it would be possible to make our 101 Bison pictures in Oklahoma, as all of the Indians, cowboys, livestock, and other paraphernalia we were using on the coast would be leaving in April to join the Miller road show. The Miller Brothers ranch was a vast spread of perhaps ten miles wide by fifteen miles long. Everything we needed for making western pictures was on that ranch, including a herd of bison, and close by was an Indian reservation where we could hire real Indians in their colorful native costumes. On a rise overlooking the layout was the Miller home. It was a mansion, painted white, and a real showplace. It was illuminated and heated by the natural gas readily available on the ranch. The oil actually oozed out of the ground in numerous places. This accessible oil eventually brought a fortune to the Miller family.

The one thing the ranch lacked as a site for making our 101 Bison pictures was the scenery we had taken for granted in the Santa Ynez Canyon in Santa Monica. This new country was as flat as a pancake and had the further disadvantage of the stormy winter months which made it impossible even to consider making such a change. Joe and his brother Zack talked it over and felt that they could get additional Indians, cowboys, and livestock, plus a couple of stagecoaches and other equipment around the ranch to make up their road show. This meant that they would have to take only their star performers from the group wintering at the coast. So we made a deal. Joe agreed to go along with me to California to straighten things out there, while Zack was to stay at the ranch to rustle things at that end. After Joe had selected what he needed from their winter quarters in Venice, California, we moved the rest of their outfit to our Santa Monica Canyon location. I persuaded Joe Miller to let Brooks stay with us, and he was put in full charge of looking after the Millers' interests as well as ours. It wasn't an easy task to arrange housing and a mess hall for the people and shelter and corrals for the livestock in such haste. Brooks helped to ease the situation by having the Indians set up their own tepee village almost at the crest of the south ridge of the canyon, and there they lived all by themselves.

About the middle of March, my partners sent Mack Sennett, Mabel Normand, Ford Sterling, Fred Mace, and Henry "Pathé" Lehrman out to California, as planned, to start making Keystone comedies. Incidentally, there have been so many conflicting dates given in interviews, autobiographies, and biographies as to the date of arrival of this group in California for the Keystone Film Company, and when the first pictures were made, the following chain of events might throw some light on the puzzle and prevent indignation on the part of serious historians.

All our western pictures were being made out at our rapidly

growing studio within the fenced-in area in Santa Ynez Canyon, where trespassing became too dangerous for the detectives of the Patents Company. This meant that our Edendale studio was idle, so we made it the permanent studio for producing our Keystone comedies. It was there that Sennett began making them, all split-reelers, about the middle of April, 1912.

A number of players was added to the company immediately, and eventually the Keystone stock company included such names as Charles Murray, Louise Fazenda, Polly Moran, Roscoe "Fatty" Arbuckle, his wife Minta Durfee Arbuckle, Charles Chaplin, Marie Dressler, Gloria Swanson, Ben Turpin, George Jeske, Peggy Pearce, Hank Mann, Heinie and Chester Conklin (not related), Phyllis Haver, Marie Prevost, Gertrude Selby, and a great many others.

One of the first split-reels made there featured Mabel Normand and it had a title something on the order of *A Water Nymph*. At any rate, Mabel wore a close-fitting overall bathing suit, similar to that worn by Annette Kellerman in her physical culture and diving pictures produced by Vitagraph around 1910. Actually, it was a gymnastic suit that covered Mabel from toe to neck but since it was skintight, it displayed her youthful figure and was quite daring for that era. The split-reelers were not necessarily released in the order in which they had been made, but an effort was made always to have two different types of background and, if possible, different players in the two comedies on the same reel. When Henry "Pathé" Lehrman saw the picture with Mabel in the bathing suit, his always nimble mind clicked. He suggested a bevy of bathing beauties for the stock company, and out of this idea grew the Mack Sennett bathing beauties. Among the early bathing beauties to join the company was a beautiful sixteen-year-old who looked enough like Mabel Normand to pass as her twin sister. She not only had the looks but a plan she thought was the path to becoming a star, and she wasted no time in displaying her charms.

Early in June the preliminary work had been completed on a combine made up of independent film companies so that they could present a solid front to fight the Patents Company. The combine was ready to be formed officially. As the secretary and treasurer of the New York Motion Picture Company, my presence in New York City was necessary. With the job of getting the Edendale studio in shape for the Keystone company to produce comedies on a regular schedule, I had delayed my departure until the last minute and arrived there just in time to attend the meetings, sign a raft of papers and documents, and hurry back to Los Angeles. I was in such a rush, in fact, that it wasn't until after I had changed trains at Chicago and was well under way on the Santa Fe that I realized I had forgotten to stop over in Chicago to keep the appointment with Donald Bell of Bell & Howell that I had made when he called me from Chicago while I was attending the business meetings in New York. It was my intention to make a selection of lenses for the camera they were completing for us for shipment to California.

I no sooner arrived in Los Angeles than a friend of mine, Jim Jeffries, the ex-heavyweight champion, who owned a very popular bar in town, sent a message that he wanted to see me right away on urgent business. As soon as Jim saw me, he came over and told me rather excitedly that a friend of his who was in a position to know had told him that some of our Keystone actors were in serious trouble because the district attorney's office planned to pick them up the next morning on a charge of contributing to the delinquency of a minor—our sixteen-year-old beauty. When he gave the the actors' names, I was stunned. The story would make fine political hay but the publicity could ruin our company. I was advised to get the actors involved out of Los Angeles quietly and across the border into Mexico as fast as I could that night and to keep them down there until things cooled off.

I managed to reach Sennett who thought it was just a gag. I had a hard time convincing him otherwise. Tijuana was just across the state line, about one hundred and fifty miles south of Los Angeles, and a good five-hour drive over the rough roads of that era. Sennett and I decided to round up the four men and pile them into my 1912 Losier touring car and send them on their way with my chauffeur, George Sherer. They reached the bridge that went into Mexico over the Rio Grande River about three o'clock in the morning and found the gate closed to vehicles for the night, so they walked across into Tijuana, which was a sunbaked town with a single, dusty street where burros roamed at will, quite different from what it is today. There was only one hotel—take it or leave it.

The next day, Sennett and I talked over the situation and decided that the best thing to do was to send the rest of the company down to Mexico to make some pictures as a cover up. We were fortunate that none of the advance publicity had mentioned a specific release date for the coming Keystone comedies. It was hotter than Hades that summer in Tijuana, and each Saturday George would drive me down with the payroll and negative stock. I would take the film that Mack had shot the previous week back to Los Angeles to be developed. The necessity for strict secrecy as to the reason for the company being in Tijuana is obvious, and when our publicity announced only that Keystone comedies would be released regularly in the fall, without an exact date, no one seemed the wiser. It doesn't seem important to me to try to clear up the conflicting dates given in various publications because that all seems so long ago, but my coauthor, as a serious historian, insisted I tell the tale of what really happened and straighten it out once and for all.

When I was in New York at the time the Keystone company was formed, I learned via the grapevine that the Patents Company planned to bring an infringement suit against each individual independent company. I suggested to Bauman that the independents would have a better chance to beat the Patents Company if they all got together and organized one big company and then issued stock to the member companies according to their assets. Bauman thought my idea was impractical and a pipe dream. It couldn't be done, he said, because each man considered himself better and more important than the other. Shortly after I returned to California, however, Bauman discussed my suggestion with Carl Laemmle, head of the Imp company, and Pat Powers, head of The Powers Company, who used Powers Picture Plays for his trademark. Laemmle and Powers were two of the smartest men in the picture business. Both thought the idea sound and went to work on it right away. They lined up a number of independents, and in June,

1912, formed the Universal Film Manufacturing Company. Charlie Bauman was chosen as the temporary president, Pat Powers as vice-president, Carl Laemmle as treasurer, and I as their general manager. Each member of the newly formed Universal company was to be issued stock in accordance with his assets. Besides the New York Motion Picture Company, there were the Imp company; The Powers Company; the Nestor company, owned by Dave Horsley; the Champion company belonging to Mark Dintenfass; Charles Jourjon's Eclair company; the Yankee company, owned by William Steiner, and William (Bill) Swanson and Joe Engel, producers of Rex pictures.

It was one big happy family for about a month after I returned to the coast. I had just completed closing the Imp studios on Boyle Heights when, at the first meeting of the new company, just what Bauman had predicted actually came to pass. Everybody in the combine wanted to be the permanent president. Bauman took the stand, and rightly so, that since we were the largest company and ours the largest block of stock, Kessel or Bauman should be the president. The opposition argued that each member company should have one vote and the man who got the majority vote would be the president. It was obvious to us that under such a procedure we had no chance of winning, so we refused to go through with the deal and pulled out. It wasn't that simple, however. All the rest of the companies that remained in the combine claimed we were committed and that all our assets and property therefore belonged to the combine, namely, the Universal company. Powers got tough and had a group of strong-arm men try to take possession of our laboratory on Nineteenth Street, New York City, the end of June, 1912, as the combine's first move.

One account dramatizes this incident out of all proportion, completely disregarding the facts. According to this version, Kessel, in response to a telephone call recruiting forces, arrived at the studio (which it was not—it was only a laboratory) and cooked hot dogs for those who were protecting the place. The author of this story goes on to say that after some shooting and slugging, the place remained under a state of seige. Actually,

Adam Kessel never set foot in the lab during the trouble and there was no shooting. What fighting there was lasted for about ten minutes. George Dobbs, who worked in the chemical room, had the misfortune to lose one eye, but no one else suffered any injury. The police arrived and put an end to the fray. Doc Willat did ask a few of the employees to stay the night and some volunteered. I can no longer remember the names of all who did but Billy Westerburg, Charlie Kipper, Jack Kelly, and Bert Seibel were among those who stayed.

Our Santa Ynez Canyon studio would have been a real prize for Universal, but since I was there at the time, I am absolutely certain no serious attempt to take it was made. Nevertheless, the same writer thought this a great opportunity to become even more dramatic. His story relates how a director strapped on a large forty-five six-shooter, took command, and had an old Civil War cannon loaded with scrap iron placed in a position to repel the enemy. If this wasn't enough of a tale, he had guards with sawed-off shotguns guarding the gates. "A clash of arms was avoided or the canyon at Santa Monica would have been running deep with gore," he wrote.

This hardly sounds sillier than what actually happened. Brooks, who was in charge of our Indians, had them dress in full regalia and cover their faces with war paint. He then asked them to parade on a ridge well in view of anyone approaching the canyon along the beach road, the only way to get in. One of the several prop cannons we used in our Indian and soldier pictures Brooks placed pointing in the direction the enemy was expected to come and had his Indians carrying army muskets and jumping and hopping in an Indian war dance. The whole thing was staged by Brooks. Some of the cowboys joined in the fun and fired their guns in the air, using blank cartridges.

While this was going on, I was swamped day after day with telegrams from Laemmle, Swanson, and Horsley, all of whom offered me considerable inducements to turn over our property out in California to the Universal company, which would have meant selling my partners down the river, as it were. When I wouldn't agree, the strategy shifted to get possession of the Edendale studio. Swanson came out to do the dirty work, stopping off en route at Denver to pick up his friend Jack Mahan to help him.

I had promised Tom McCarey, father of the now-famous director Leo McCarey, that I would arrange to photograph the lightweight championship fight between Ad Wolgast, the title-holder, and Joe Rivers, the challenger, to be held at McCarey's fight arena in Vernon, California, on July 4, 1912, which was only a few days away. The new development, the arrival of Swanson and his guerillas, created some apprehension. I thought that they might try to grab the three cameras I had planned to use in photographing the fight. I explained the situation to Tom McCarey and to Wolgast's manager, Tom Jones. They assured me that anyone who attempted to get near the camera-shooting platform would be well taken care of before the fight.

After the attempt by Universal to take possession of our laboratory in New York the previous week, my attorney, Frank Graham, had advised placing a guard around the Edendale studio for protection. I organized a so-called police force with Fred Mace as the head and told him to act as chief. I gave him strict orders not to let anybody in unless he knew them, and not to leave the premises without making sure that all the doors and windows were locked.

On either July second or third, while I was at the fight arena arranging the platform for the three cameras, the smooth operator, Bill Swanson, aware that the Keystone company was still down in Tijuana shooting pictures, thought that this was the ideal time to take over the Edendale studio. Swanson, backed up by Mahan, a bushy-haired gorilla-like character, and some other roughnecks, began his dirty work. He went to the main entrance and naturally Mace did not know him. Swanson had timed his visit knowing that I wasn't there and made use of a ruse as old as the hills. He asked Mace if I were around. Mace told him I was not. Swanson said he was an old friend of mine from New York and could he make a telephone call. Mace, completely taken in, said "Sure," and unlocked the door. At that moment, Mahan and his goons materialized from somewhere, manhandled Mace and the guards and took possession. Swanson attached his own padlocks to all the doors and warned Mace that if he or anyone else tampered with the new locks they would be guilty of breaking the law. Quite satisfied with this maneuver, Swanson and his henchmen left.

Everything was set at the fight arena so I drove over to the Santa Monica studio where Mace reached me by phone and told me what had happened. I drove to the Edendale studio as fast as I could. When I got there, I gave orders to "knock the damn lock off." "You can't do that," Mace replied. "Who's going to stop me," I wanted to know. "They will," Mace said. "Did they show you a writ or court order giving them possession?" I demanded. "You're a helluva police chief," I said. "Get me a sledgehammer and I'll knock all the locks off. We'll repossess the studio." And we did.

The afternoon of the prizefight, McCarey had more than a dozen roughnecks surrounding the camera platform. Swanson and his boys were there to see the fight but never made any attempt to bother me. The camera operators were Ray Smallwood and Walter Wright, while I handled the third one. About five minutes before the bout commenced, I saw, from my high vantage point, Tom McCarey leading Mack Sennett through the crowd. Sennett had driven up from Tijuana at the last minute to see the fight. He sat on the platform with us, his long legs dangling over the edge.

It was a savage fight that ended in the thirteenth round in what appeared to be a double knockout when both went down. Rivers fell flat on his back with Wolgast on top of him. Walsh, the referee, raised Wolgast off Rivers with one hand, while he counted Rivers out with the other. There was considerable yelling and booing, but what most people didn't see, the camera did. Wolgast had Rivers in one corner of the ring as he pounded away at his midsection until Rivers went down. As Rivers fell flat on his back, he raised his knee in agony just as Wolgast, carried on by the momentum of his two-fisted attack, fell on top of him and was struck accidentally in the groin by Rivers' knee, which knocked the breath out of him. The referee saw what had happened and acted accordingly.

In spite of all of our differences, Bill Swanson and I remained good friends. We continued to have dinner together, more often at Levy's famous restaurant in downtown Los Angeles, or at Baron Long's Country Club in Vernon, some five miles south of the city. Time and again Swanson tried to swing me over to his side, stressing the fact that I had been named general manager of the Universal company when it was formed and that I would get a bonus and a fat block of stock if I'd desert my partners and join them. Of course I turned his proposition down, but I couldn't help wondering why he made me such a generous offer, for I couldn't imagine how I could be that important to them. It wasn't long before I knew the answer.

Toward the end of July, 1912, Carl Laemmle was elected permanent president of Universal, with Pat Powers retaining his job as vice-president. Once more Swanson tried to make a deal with me and, when I told him I would stick with my partners, Universal brought suit against us in Los Angeles, with Swanson as their representative here. Both Kessel and Bauman came out from New York for the trial, and when Sennett heard they were here, he came up from Tijuana where they were still busy producing comedies since charges were still open against those few but important actors.

When Mack arrived in Los Angeles, he demanded to know when we were going to release the split-reelers he had been making. Neither Kessel nor Bauman was in any mood to be questioned about anything. In addition to the coming Universal suit, they were quite annoyed at what Bauman called the "stinking mess" at the Edendale studio that had made it vital for the company to hide out in Mexico while making pictures. Sennett got a little hot under the collar as he had had nothing to do with creating the situation. I told Bauman it had been my suggestion that the company go down to Tijuana and that Mack had agreed. It seemed a good move to protect the brand-new company. Bauman was worried about Universal publicity boys getting the real dope on why the company was in Mexico. He figured that if they found out they would have no trouble at all in getting headlines in all the papers that might very well put the Keystone company, which hadn't yet released a picture, out of business before it could even get launched. Finally Bau-

man told Mack bluntly that no Keystone comedies would be
released until things were settled and there was no possible
chance of a scandal. It was agreed that we would keep putting
out publicity on the forthcoming Keystone comedies but would
hold off naming an actual release date until we were absolutely
sure everything was settled.

Late in August Sennett and the company returned from
Tijuana to work in the Edendale studio, and the first of the
Keystone regular weekly releases, which had been made in the
spring, came out on September 23, 1912.

The Universal company had an array of lawyers for the trial,
headed by a big-time lawyer of the Southern Pacific Railroad,
while we retained Hunsaker and Hunsaker as well as my personal lawyer, Frank Graham. It was a hotly contested battle,
and it looked like we were going to lose until Graham accidentally discovered that I, as secretary-treasurer of the New
York Motion Picture Company, had not signed that particular
part of the contract where we agreed to transfer our company
assets to the Universal company in exchange for stock. Our attorneys claimed that without my signature the contract was
null and void. In the end, we did not have to turn the company
over to Universal for stock, but they did win from us the right
to use the brand name Bison films. None of us had realized that
I hadn't signed part of the contract, but evidently the opposition knew, and no doubt that was why Swanson tried so hard
to win me over to their side before bringing suit against us.

As I thought about it, the circumstances that caused me to
miss signing part of the contract came back to me. While we
were all assembled with the attorneys for Universal in New
York on the day of the signing, documents were being passed
like a deck of cards around the long table where we sat. There
were numerous documents to be signed and near the end I
was called out of the room to take a long distance telephone
call from Chicago. It was Donald Bell who wanted to know
if I had made a decision as to what make and focal length
lenses I would like to have on the camera I had ordered for
the New York Motion Picture Company in March. With the
meeting that was taking place in the other room on my mind, I

found it impossible to concentrate on the conversation about
lenses, so I made an appointment to stop off and see Bell in
Chicago on my trip back to the coast. (As I mentioned earlier,
I completely forgot to stop.) When I returned to the meeting
some minutes later, the signing was all over and everybody
was shaking hands like long-lost brothers, while the attorneys
gathered up the signed documents. Later, when my missing
signature became an issue, Bauman remembered that someone
had asked him if I had signed everything and he, not having
noticed my absence from the room, assured him that I had.

Swanson, who had stayed in California to look for a site on
which to establish a west coast studio for Universal, found one
that he liked on Lankershim Boulevard, ten miles northwest
of Los Angeles, where the Universal studios are today. In spite
of the Universal suit, we had remained friends and Swanson
seemed to rely a good deal on my judgment. At any rate, he
set a day for us to drive out to look at the site he had chosen.
I didn't like the location and gave him plenty of reasons why
not. Besides being out in the sticks, the roads were so bad
that it took a couple of hours to drive out there. Cahuenga
Boulevard, leading from the little town of Hollywood to
Lankershim Boulevard, was about three miles of tough going
over a narrow dirt road with ruts so deep that once the wheels
of a car got into them they stayed right there until the car
reached the top of the grade.

At that time few, if any, movie people lived in Hollywood,
and the furnishings, props, and all the other things required
to make moving pictures would have to be carted all the way
from downtown Los Angeles. I was not the only person to point
this out to Swanson, but he went ahead anyway. Laemmle
came out sometime later and put his stamp of approval on the
property. It took about two years from the time Swanson chose
the site to complete the studio.

In November or December, 1913, Charles Chaplin joined
the Keystone company. According to my partners, he was
playing in New York in a vaudeville act called "A Night in An
English Music Hall" when Kessel's brother, Charlie, saw him
and thought Chaplin was so funny he couldn't get to the office

quickly enough the next morning to tell them about it. Kessel and Bauman offered Chaplin seventy-five dollars a week, which was far more than he was making, and this was the start of one of the most fabulous careers in the motion picture business. Chaplin accepted the offer and was sent out to Sennett on the coast, who did not savvy this little English comic at all for quite some time, any more than most of the Keystone actors did.

Chaplin knew nothing about acting in films and was lost among such accomplished scene stealers as Ford Sterling, Fred Mace, and Charles Murray, who didn't go out of their way to help him any. Mabel Normand, however, did all she could to help him, coaching and encouraging him. One day, during his first few months on the Keystone lot, Charlie came to me and said he felt like quitting and going back on the stage. I must admit that I didn't try to talk him out of it. It appears that his famous tramp outfit—the derby hat, baggy pants, oversized shoes, flexible cane, and small mustache—came about accidentally when Lehrman, who was directing Charlie in a picture, asked him to play the part of a tramp. Chaplin, with Lehrman's help, quickly assembled the costume, using clothes borrowed from the other Keystone actors.

It wasn't until November, 1914, however, that Charlie Chaplin really came into his own when he played with Marie Dressler and Mabel Normand in a comedy called *Tillie's Punctured Romance*. This five-reel slapstick comedy gave him his opportunity, and from then on he began to be recognized as an outstanding comic.

When we lost the right to use the brand name Bison films to the Universal company, we rechristened the same unit Broncho films, but they never were as popular as the original 101 Bisons, and we lost quite a bit of business. We had two other western units operating at our Santa Monica mountain studio, namely, the Kaybee and Domino films.

In the meantime, the Patents Company had brought suit against the New York Motion Picture Company in New York City. But the powerful "movie trust" was a thing of the past because the government was by now strongly antitrust. The

Patents Company apparently saw the handwriting on the wall and did not press the suit. As a matter of fact, the Patents Company finally was ordered to dissolve early in 1915.

Although Carl Laemmle was president of Universal, Pat Powers and Bill Swanson both wanted that office, and the battle still raged, with Horsley waiting to hop on the bandwagon. Eventually Laemmle acquired the necessary financial backing to buy out Powers, and then Swanson, who told me that he got $750,000 for his stock, while Powers was paid a cool million for his. Laemmle thus became the permanent president. He later bought out the rest of the stockholders, but not at the price he had paid to Powers and Swanson.

Late in 1913 my partners, Kessel and Bauman, met a bright boy from Wall Street by the name of Harry Aitkin, who sold them on the idea of making a lot of money fast in the moving picture business. It was their plan to form the Triangle Picture Company, incorporate for a couple of million dollars or more, and sell stock to the public. Knowing the background of my partners, Kessel and Bauman, I could understand the appeal such a proposition would have for them.

My background in the film business was picture-making and selling stock to the public was completely out of my line. I told my partners so, and that my share of our partnership in the New York Motion Picture Company could not be pooled in such a scheme. I had money and additional backing and offered to buy them out, but they wouldn't sell. Intuition told me that things had come so easy for them in the movie business that over-confidence had replaced their old down-to-earth manner of doing business. The outcome was easy to predict. In the end, they bought me out for one hundred thousand dollars, and this was the finish of a partnership of three men who had gone through thick and thin together, starting with practically nothing, and who now had one of the most successful companies in the business.

Miss Kenny, to whom we had given the odd share of stock when we formed the New York Motion Picture Company in the spring of 1909, turned that share in for Triangle stock and, a short while later, sold her holdings for ten thousand dollars. It was obvious that there was some fast maneuvering somewhere.

Triangle folded some years later amid talk of a stock scandal and all sorts of other rumors. Charlie Bauman told me a few years after the thing blew up (he liked to boast, you know), that when the Triangle was incorporated, the New York Motion Picture Company's and the Keystone Film Company's assets were represented at far beyond their real value. By some error, the Santa Monica mountain property that we leased and where we shot our westerns was understood to be owned by the New York Motion Picture Company and registered as an asset. The result was that they were accused of selling watered stock. There was quite a commotion about it, and, in the end, he and Kessel were practically broke after paying a raft of lawyers to keep them out of jail.

Griffith, Ince, and Sennett, whose names were used to promote the sale of stock, were totally unaware of what had been going on and were not dragged into the case. Each went his respective way when the scheme blew up. Thus did Adam Kessel and Charles O. Bauman, two men who helped establish the movie industry we all enjoy today, exit from that world.

Chapter 9

THE PERILS OF PAULINE

ALTHOUGH I ENJOYED making the Pathé news subjects a great deal, it had been my hope ever since I left Porter and the Rex company to return to photographing production, but when I was assigned to shoot *The Perils of Pauline,* I never had the slightest inkling that the serial would be remembered by motion picture historians more than fifty years later. It is for this group that some of the facts are recorded. *Pauline* was made at the Pathé studio located at 1 Congress Street, Jersey City Heights, during 1914. The main entrance to the Pathé studio was on the corner of Congress Street and Webster Avenue. The studio itself consisted of a lower and an upper stage. The upper stage was equipped with a tank about 30′ x 30′ square and 8′ deep. We could lower a fair-sized set inch by inch into the water when shooting such suspense scenes as a dungeon gradually being flooded with water, leaving the heroine helpless, but you could be sure she would be rescued at the beginning of the next episode. The top and sides of both stages were made of small panes of clear glass, much on the order of a garden greenhouse. White and black diffusers inside covered the top and side of each stage and were controlled at will by pulling cords that hung at the sides. Arc lights and Cooper-Hewitt mercury tubes were used to mix with the soft daylight for photographing. Constructed in 1910, the studio was one of the most modern and well-equipped of the time.

Lower stage of the Pathé studio showing the glass sides and top, with the white muslin diffusers, black cloth draw curtains, and the hanging arc lights. No Cooper-Hewitt mercury floor lights are shown in the picture. Man at the camera is Arthur Miller.

The Perils of Pauline was duped and used in showings for many different purposes. Charles Goddard even wrote a novel of the same title in 1914 and used still pictures from the serial as illustrations for it. The original intention of keeping the audience in suspense from week to week was forgotten. In one instance, the entire serial was recut to make each episode a complete story in itself, whereas the original idea had been to leave either the hero or heroine in a rather precarious predicament at the end of each episode, thereby guaranteeing the return of the audience, anxious to know how they were rescued from the clutches of the villain. This "cliffhanger" idea was used for the first ten episodes. It succeeded so well that another ten were added, so that twenty episodes in all of *The Perils of Pauline* were produced.

The man in full charge of *Pauline* as well as of the Pathé studio was Louis J. Gasnier, who directed the first ten episodes but then turned the director's job over to Donald MacKenzie. Donald MacKenzie had played the part of a pirate in one of the early installments. Shooting scripts were written by George B. Seitz and Bertram Millhauser. Seitz always cut the finished episodes. Contrary to many serials produced afterwards, each installment was completed separately. Later, many were made as one picture, shooting every location, from the first to the last episode, in one visit. The interiors were handled in the same manner—serials produced on a sort of production-line basis.

Photographing *The Perils of Pauline* was my assignment, and my second cameraman, as they called them then, was Harry Wood. The very nature of the serial called for peril and dangerous situations, and frequently required extra cameras to shoot several angles of a particular stunt. Cameramen working at the studio who happened to be between assignments operated the extra cameras.

We used negative film manufactured by the Pathé company. Gasnier viewed the developed negative on the screen and chose the desired take of each scene. Aside from the directors, the principal players, and the camera crew, three men deserve special credit for their part in making *Pauline*. One was Frank Redman, Sr., who was the head of the property department. He also played many small parts. Teamed together were two young fellows whose last names, I am ashamed to admit I never knew, but one was called Pitch and the other Cooney. Both played bit parts when necessary and did the work of property men, as well as what would be the work of a grip today — handling camera dollies, reflectors, dolly tracks, and so on. The many times I was perched on a platform or rigged on an automobile in front of the radiator I felt perfectly safe as I had full confidence in their ability and judgment. One of their most important jobs was to figure out and rig stunts that required the use of piano wire — often a life depended on their skill.

Toward the end of the serial, Spencer Bennett, now a director, was made an assistant to Donald MacKenzie and also played parts when called upon. The principals in the cast, of course, were Pearl White, Crane Wilbur, and Paul Panzer, who played the villain. I have had hundreds of inquiries about these three personalities, especially Pearl, and can only describe them as they were when we worked together. I have no reason to believe they were any different from other people. Like other movie stars, it was difficult for them to have any privacy. They were mobbed in public just as all the famous stars who followed. It seems to me that there was more cooperation from performers in those days than there is now, and to pile in a car and go on a day's location was like going on a picnic, for all hands worked in harmony. It is true that we didn't have dolly shots to make, no sound equipment to bother about, and everything in general was much less complicated, which could account for much less strain. Most of our locations were around Fort Lee, Coytesville, and among the rocky cliffs of the Palisades, as well as a little farther up the Hudson River in the town of Englewood, where we made use of the Browning and Morrow estates as "homes" of characters in the cast.

Under Rambo's grape arbor, mentioned earlier in the book, remained the place to eat lunch, and the menu was still ham and eggs, coffee, and apple pie. We rented such automobiles as a Thomas touring car, an Abbot Detroit, a Buick, and a Rambler from Mereo's garage on Hudson Boulevard. The cameraman always rode in the front beside the driver, the most convenient place for him to rest the Pathé camera on the floor between his legs for safety while in transit. The tripod was carried in a fixed bracket attached to the running board of the car.

Pearl White was a trim, attractive girl and her pleasant, unaffected manner made her a joy to work with. She saved all of her acting for in front of the camera and otherwise was never anything but herself. She had begun acting on the stage at the age of four. About 1910 her motion picture career started when she went with the Powers Picture Players studio. I have been told that she performed with a circus and she learned then the acrobatics which enabled her to do all her own stunts in *Pauline*. During the time I knew her, Pearl often talked of her days with road shows doing one-night stands in "tank towns" as she called them, but never did I hear her say she had performed with a circus. I am positive that she was neither an acrobat nor a tumbler.

Pearl claimed it was Irving Cummings, one of the leading men with the Powers company, who was responsible for her being in the movies. He and Pearl had traveled in some road shows together, and he persuaded Pat Powers to add her to the Powers stock company. Irving Cummings and Jack Standing were leading men at the Pathé studio in 1913. Later, in 1938, Irving Cummings directed *Little Miss Broadway*, starring Shirley Temple with George Murphy (now senator) as leading man, and I photographed it.

To go back a little, before Pat Powers entered the movie business he was in some way connected with the phonograph manufacturing industry, and in the early days when the Patents Company was exerting all the pressure it could to protect its monopoly, Powers, known as the "Fighting Irishman," openly declared that no one was going to stop him from making moving pictures. It was he who encouraged, and some said financed, Joe Bianchi, who was a first-class tool and dye maker employed by the Columbia Phonograph Company, to build a moving picture camera that would circumvent the Edison patents. Before the camera was finished, the Columbia Phonograph Company became interested and believed so strongly in its eventual success that they set up a licensing organization designed to compete with the Patents Company. Some of the independents tried to take advantage of the situation by claiming they were making their pictures under the new Columbia licensing organization, but the only one who really did was the newly formed Thanhouser company. In 1910, Thanhouser converted the New Rochelle Skating Rink into a studio. When the Bianchi camera was ready to be tested, it proved to be a failure, like a good many tries before it. The Thanhouser company, however, continued to make their pictures in New Rochelle, enduring the same harassment from the Patents Company as the rest of the independents.

Crane Wilbur was a handsome young man of the matinee-

idol type. He had a full head of dark hair with a natural
wave, and his charm on and off the screen left the girls swoon-
ing. Paul Panzer, I thought, was perfect in his role of the
eager-to-help-type of villain who unsuspectingly laid the plans
for the dirty work to enable him to gain the favor of the heroine.
Today this kind of broad plotting and planning would be considered the worst kind of corn, but at the time of *The Perils
of Pauline* the audience really went for it in a big way. Panzer
was a friendly man, one of the very early moving picture actors,
and I think that he took his acting career far more seriously
than either Pearl White or Crane Wilbur ever did.

Each episode of *Pauline* took about two weeks to make and
about the time the eighth episode was out, someone wrote a
song called "Poor Pauline." Perhaps this was the start of
personal appearances, as Pearl appeared at some of the nicer
movie houses. This created a demand for Crane Wilbur, and
he gave dramatic recitations at each of his personal appearances. Both were a big hit every time.

I have been asked time and again whether Pearl White performed all the daredevil stunts that occurred in the serial or if
doubles were used. Common sense should indicate that if either
Pearl or Crane Wilbur had been injured doing these often
dangerous stunts, the serial would be out of business, but there
were times when both performed hazardous stunts at their
own stubborn insistence. I remember a stunt from one of the
early episodes that was not considered to be dangerous — just
the transfer from the running board of one moving automobile
to another, also in motion. The cars didn't have to move very
fast, as under-cranking the camera created the illusion of high
speed for both cars. Pearl struggled free of her captors, got out
on the running board of the car, but as she reached for the
other automobile traveling alongside that was to rescue her, she
somehow lost her footing and fell between the moving cars.
Only the quick thinking of the two drivers who turned their
cars out and apart prevented a serious accident.

I think Crane Wilbur was more adamant than Pearl about
doing his own stunts, especially those that concerned swimming
or diving, as he was an expert at both. In my opinion, it was

foolhardy for either of them to take chances when they were too far from the camera to be identified.

On one occasion we went to upstate New York on location in order to capture the beauty of Ausable Chasm. Over the centuries, a river had cut high, rugged cliffs that towered straight up on both sides through the chasm, and we played many scenes against this beautiful scenery in the background. Just how the situation arose in the story, I cannot recall, but the hero was called upon to dive from one of the rocks that jutted out from the chasm wall, about forty or fifty feet high, into the water below. I am sure that Wilbur knew the camera was too far away for him to be recognized. Nevertheless, he insisted on making the dive himself and would have it no other way. After we shot the scene, which went off without a hitch, I wondered if that wasn't the way it was supposed to be. Wilbur knew precisely what he was doing and probably saved some trouble, if not actual injury, for the double, Pitch, who rarely took the time to plan his own stunts carefully.

Another time when both Pitch and Cooney, doubling for Pearl and Wilbur, jumped from a rocky cliff into Lake Saranac below they missed, by only a small margin, bouncing off the sharp rocks they passed on the way down. There was no such person as a professional stunt man in those days. There was an individual named Rodman Law who did crazy things, like jumping off the Brooklyn Bridge. His sister, Ruth, performed similar daring feats, but all they got for it was their names in the newspapers. The present-day professional stunt man makes every effort to plan his stunt so that it will provide the least amount of risk. Even so, every now and then, things fail to work as scheduled.

To sum up, both Pearl White and Crane Wilbur did stunts and sometimes took unnecessary chances. But there were occasions when it would have been absolutely crazy for them to perform the stunts themselves. Of one thing I am certain and that is they both did more dangerous stunts than any performer does today. Using a double is common practice now, and it makes far more sense than the dangerous system that prevailed in the early days.

With all the daredevil thrills and stunts that took place during the course of making the serial, we were indeed fortunate
never to experience a serious accident, although there were
several narrow escapes. One of these involved a balloon. The
so-called airfield was on Staten Island, where a fellow named
Leo Stevens kept his biplane. While George Seitz was visiting
us at the airfield, he discovered that Stevens also owned a
balloon, and by the time we had finished the aeroplane chapter, he had written the next one around the balloon. The day
came when we were working among the rocky cliffs of the
Palisades near the town of Coytesville, shooting scenes with
the inflated balloon with the square basket hanging from its
base. I can't recall the sequence of the scenes but I do remember there were some close-ups of Pearl in the basket to be made.
The basket was held fast to the rocks of the Palisades by a one-
inch manila rope fastened to it. When we had finished the
close shots, Leo Stevens, owner of the balloon, climbed into
the basket with Pearl and directed the paying out of the rope
until it was at its end, held fast with the same type of anchor
as is used on a boat, which kept the balloon about seventy-five
feet in the air. Stevens ducked down out of sight of the camera,
so we could begin taking shots of the balloon. At the bottom
of the picture, Pearl could be seen as she looked over the edge
of the basket with the large inflated balloon above against the
sky making an imposing composition.

Suddenly some rocks began to tumble, loosening the anchor,
and before anyone could do anything except to stand there
in amazement, the balloon gained altitude and slowly drifted
up and over the Hudson River toward New York with its
anchor still dangling from the end of the rope. There were no
high buildings in uptown New York at that time. If I remember correctly, the highest building was the Woolworth building and that was near the southern tip of Manhattan.

We had no choice except to pack the equipment and to
return to the studio to await information. Since this was an
unscheduled balloon flight, those who saw it had no idea who
or what was in the balloon. It took off about eleven in the
morning and it wasn't until five o'clock in the afternoon that

someone called the studio to tell Gasnier that Pearl was safe and on her way back to New York from somewhere in Philadelphia, where they had landed. The next day I asked Pearl if she was frightened during the balloon trip. Her answer was that what upset her most was that the owner of the airship kept repeating that it wasn't equipped to fly, that it didn't have a rip cord, making it impossible to open the valve at the neck of the balloon which would deflate the bag and allow it to descend. Pearl said that when Stevens saw a large patch of open ground below, he climbed up the shrouds, held his nose with one hand to protect himself from the escaping gas and released the valve with the other. As the balloon got closer to the ground, Pearl said, the basket began to swing back and forth, finally hitting the ground rather hard. Pearl averred though, that taking everything into consideration, she wouldn't have missed that trip for anything.

After concluding the foregoing about *The Perils of Pauline*, I came across a book which purports to relate the history of the movie serials. I have read many criticisms of films made in the early days, but for the first time has a would-be historian called the work of someone "crude," when as a matter of fact, he makes it clear in doing so that he hasn't the slightest knowledge of what he is criticizing. He also states that most of the people who were in the middle of things during what he calls "those glorious days" are gone forever and their memories unrecorded. It may come as a surprise to him that I, who photographed *The Perils of Pauline*, am very much alive and feel compelled to straighten out a few things. Our friend goes on to say that he considers the language used in the subtitles an unforgiveable crime for it was so bad even children laughed at it. He apparently believes the reason for this was that the producer, Louis Gasnier, was French. It is amazing to me how anyone who sets out to write a history of the serials wouldn't be aware that the man who made more serials with Pearl White than anyone else was George B. Seitz, a well-educated man. It was Seitz, together with Bertram Millhauser, who wrote each episode of *Pauline*, edited them, and wrote the subtitles. After each episode was completed, someone on the staff of the Hearst

Typical shots from
The Perils of Pauline.
(Cameraman on car-mounted
platform is Arthur Miller.)

newspapers would look at it on the screen so that he could write the story for the Sunday supplement. It seems rather naive of our author to believe that all of these writers were illiterate. If the reason for ungrammatical subtitles on what must be at the least fourth of fifth duplicate prints, very likely in 16mm, is so obscure, perhaps it is worth the space to explain what actually went on.

In 1916 I tried for personal reasons to obtain a print of one of the episodes of *The Perils of Pauline* and was told by Louis Gasnier that the negative had been shipped to France. Even before that time, the serial had been a big hit in France, and Pearl White became as popular there as she was in America. After the disastrous fire that took the lives of 180 of the cream of French society in the early days of motion pictures, the French government had passed and strictly enforced a law providing that all projection machines must be enclosed in a fireproof booth. In 1912 the Lumière Brothers placed on the market what was known as "safety" film, and for showing this film a booth was not required. The film, 28mm in width, became known in France as the "educational" film size. *The Perils of Pauline* was in such demand that a duped negative in 28mm size was made. No one knows how many prints were sold that were shown throughout the countryside in tent shows and other places. Of course, the English titles were translated by a French translator and naturally took on a French flavor.

Several years after World War I, American film historians began to be interested in *The Perils of Pauline,* since it was the first American serial. The original negative could no longer be found, and as no 35mm prints were located, it was therefore presumed that they had been destroyed in order to retrieve whatever silver hadn't been removed during the original processing. The French, with their sharp eye for business, gathered some of the 28mm prints and retranslated the French-flavored titles back to what they considered was good English usage. It is true that the results often were funny, but everybody interested knew what had happened. Such prints as found their way back to the United States were again duped to 16mm film. In some instances, the duped negative was blown up to

35mm and reduction 16mm prints made, one of which I have. It is a wonder that anything could be salvaged after the many duping stages *The Perils of Pauline* went through.

We finished photographing *The Perils of Pauline* some time before the end of the year, and my next assignment was to photograph a picture directed by a man named Verno, a Frenchman who had come to the United States to work for the Eclair company in Fort Lee. This was his first picture for the Pathé company. In little more than a week he was replaced by Frank Powell. While we were making the picture, I became intrigued with Powell's brand-new Overland racing model automobile. It was the best-looking sports car imaginable, with two bucket seats and a round gas tank placed crosswise in back of the seats. Chrome plating wasn't the thing then, but the car was trimmed with shiny brass acetylene headlights. The supply tank was fastened on one of the running boards. The car had a large brass horn connected to a flexible brass tube with a rubber bulb at the end, that produced a deep-throated honk-honk. The Overland was a shiny blue color with a leather strap over the hood of the engine. The cut-out, which could be opened legally then, made such a racket that the car could be heard a quarter of a mile before it was visible.

When we were on location, we usually quit at about three so that our director could take a little spin in his Overland roadster. Even when working in the studio, we would stop at about the same time. Powell and I would pile into his Overland and take off in search of new locations. We always took the same route, up the Hudson Boulevard to Nungesser's roadhouse, onto Anderson Avenue, up to Fort Lee, and finally up Lemoyne Avenue to the Villa Richard. The Villa Richard was a roadhouse and French restaurant about three miles from Coytesville that was perched on the edge of the Palisades overlooking the Hudson River. There Powell and I had our customary drink as we sat and gazed out the window at the superb view for a little while before driving back to the studio.

All of this took place during the month of February when it was really cold. I soon learned to come to work prepared with extra clothing for our three o'clock jaunt. At the studio

one day, the director introduced me to a visitor by the name
of Louis Mill, who seemed to be extremely interested in the
activity on the set. After a few visits, we started talking about
picture-making, and Mr. Mill invited me to have dinner with
him at his hotel in New York. During our meal he explained
that he was going to start a moving picture producing company
in Detroit and that his wife, also present, was going to do the
directing under the stage name of Cora Adams. He felt sure
that her long experience on the stage more than qualified her
for that job. It was their plan to star a young matinee idol,
Norman Hackett, and for their supporting casts, they intended
to use actors from a stock company that was playing on Wood-
ward Avenue in Detroit at the Avenue Theater. Mill told me
that a studio and laboratory already existed, set up by another
company, but that it was now idle. He thought it would be
something to start with, and there would be time to fix whatever I thought was necessary. Mill seemed to know what he
was talking about and at last offered me a contract, the first
I ever had. It sounded good, for the contract was to run for
one year and, what made it sound even better, the salary was
to be seventy-five dollars per week, plus living expenses. Pathé
News Weekly paid me thirty-five dollars. When I was trans-
ferred to *The Perils of Pauline*, the salary remained the same
but I lost my expense account, no small matter in those years.
I thought Mill's offer over a few days and then signed a contract with the Esperanto Film Company of Detroit, effective
as of March 15, 1915.

When I began working on *The Perils of Pauline*, the Pathé
studio had supplied me with a brand-new Pathé studio model
camera and tripod, plus all the trimmings, which I now collected together and placed neatly in my locker in the camera
room upstairs. Then I gathered my courage and proceeded to
the unpleasant task of telling Paul Fisher, Louis Gasnier's
second in command, that I was leaving. Fisher was very
pleasant after he heard my story and wished me well on my
new job. He asked me if I would wait for about half an hour
so that he could make out my salary check in order to save
me the trouble of another trip to the studio. In a little while

Mr. Fisher called me into his office, handed me a check for the full week's salary of thirty-five dollars, and then gave me the surprise of my life. The brand-new camera that Pathé had supplied me with when I started on *The Perils of Pauline* was mine — the studio had been deducting twenty-five dollars a week from my salary of sixty dollars to pay for it, of which I was totally unaware. The cost of the camera outfit was about nine hundred dollars (all the work done on the camera in the shop was not charged) and by mistake, the bookkeeping department had continued to deduct the twenty-five dollars each week after the camera had been paid for in full. After explaining this in great detail, Mr. Fisher handed me another check for two hundred dollars, the amount that mistakenly had been withheld. We shook hands on this happy note, and I went back upstairs to the camera room, picked up the camera, and left the studio the proud owner of a complete Pathé camera outfit. Within about three weeks, I was on my way to Detroit where I was to be the cameraman as well as do the laboratory work for the Esperanto Film Company.

Chapter 10

THE STERLING FILM COMPANY
AND ACTOR TROUBLES

FTER SEVERING MY CONNECTION with the New York Motion Picture Company, I immediately started planning a producing company of my own. There never had been any bad feeling between those in the Universal combine and me so I made a trip to New York to see if I could arrange a deal for Universal to release the pictures I intended to produce. Carl Laemmle, I knew, admired the stand I had taken not to sell stock to the public when Bauman and Kessel were forming the Triangle company, and he was most receptive to the idea of their releasing any pictures I might produce. It was Laemmle's opinion that the Universal program needed a comedy series to round out its schedule. I told him I believed that I could get Mabel Normand, Ford Sterling, or Charlie Chaplin away from Keystone to star in a series. From his slight reaction, I gathered he doubted my statement which he had every reason to. He, like nearly everyone else in the business, took for granted that the persons whose names I had mentioned were all under contract, but as a former member of the company, I was one of the few who knew differently.

Laemmle didn't think Chaplin was important enough to star, but he finally agreed that he would have the Universal lawyers draw up a contract, under the terms of which Universal would release any comedies I might make, provided they

starred either Mabel Normand or Ford Sterling. It took three
or four days for the lawyers to get a contract ready and I spent
the time visiting old friends.

I must admit that I became a little tired of explaining what
had happened between Kessel, Bauman, and me. This was now
past history as far as I was concerned, and I would rather
have discussed my future plans. Somebody told me that my
protegé, Arthur Miller, was now working for the Pathé company as a news weekly cameraman. I made the trip over to
Jersey City Heights to see him only to find that he was out
on the road which rather disappointed me. The trip wasn't
entirely wasted, however, for while I was at the studio I met
another old friend who took me on a thoroughly enjoyable
tour of the place. That trip turned out to be a sort of sentimen-
tal journey, for once I was on the Jersey side of the Hudson
I couldn't resist going north to Fort Lee and Coytesville to look
around the old haunts. Fort Lee hadn't changed much. The
Eclair company had come over from France to build a studio
on Linwood Avenue while the World-Peerless studio was just
being built up the hill on Main Street. In 1914 there was still
a lot of picture-making activity in Coytesville and, of course,
Rambo's roadhouse was as busy as ever dispensing its un-
changing menu of ham and eggs, apple pie and coffee.

As soon as I picked up the contract from the Universal
lawyers, I headed back to Los Angeles, where I missed signing
Mabel Normand by a cat's whisker. Someone had tipped off
Sennett as to my plans. Very few knew that Mabel had no
contract with the New York Motion Picture Company, owners
of the Keystone company, and only a half dozen knew I was
trying to get her to sign on the dotted line, so I had a pretty
good idea who was responsible for telling Sennett what I had
in mind. No one, however, had any idea that I was also after
Ford Sterling, and before anyone found out, I had him signed
to a contract. While I was about it, I signed "Pathé" Lehrman
as my director. "Pathé" was not really his name. In the early
days, Lehrman had bluffed his way into the Biograph studio
with a cock-and-bull story of having been a comedy director for
Pathé Frères in France. When it became apparent that this

was a tall tale, everybody jokingly began to call him "Pathé" Lehrman and the name stuck.

At the same time, I also signed about twenty other Keystone players — Louise Fazenda, Peggy Pearce, Bob Thornby, George Jeske, Chester Franklyn, Beverly Griffith, and several of the Keystone cops. Billy Jacobs, Carmen LaRue, and Olive Johnson headed up a child comedy series that I assigned to Bob Thornby to direct. My wholesale grab of Keystone players, as well as their best comedy director Pathé Lehrman, brought Kessel and Bauman hightailing it out in a hurry for a powwow with Sennett, and they made a pretty unhappy trio.

In February, 1914, I incorporated the Sterling Film Company. The name was chosen solely on the basis of Sterling's popularity. It was a nice feeling to be the sole owner and to have the freedom to make decisions without first consulting partners. The former Horsley studio at the corner of Sunset Boulevard and Gower Street was vacant, and my efforts in trying to lease it led to my buying it for $11,000. The terms were $500 down, with payments of $125 a month for the next seven years or so. If I remember correctly, the frontage on Sunset Boulevard amounted to 180 feet, with 280 feet on the Gower Street side, north toward Hollywood Boulevard. There was an old green-painted wooden fence about six feet high enclosing the property. The studio itself was ready to walk into and start making moving pictures.

Ford Sterling, of German descent, was tall, dark and well built. He was in his late twenties, a good comedian, though like many comedians, he craved to do more serious drama. Lehrman had been born in Austria of Jewish-Austrian parents, was then in his early thirties and a good director of comedies. Sterling was to be paid $250 a week, Lehrman was to get $200, and I planned to cut them in on the profits.

The contract I had with Universal worked out fine for we started making money right away. Everything was so rosy that I declared a dividend at the end of four months from the day we started shooting pictures. Sterling's cut was $1,200 and Lehrman's share amounted to $1,000. Declaring a dividend so soon was a huge mistake. The money went to their heads

In 1911 Blondeau's Tavern on the corner of Sunset Boulevard and Gower Street was transformed by David Horsley into the first moving picture studio in Hollywood for his Nestor Company. The tavern became offices and dressing rooms with a small laboratory while an open air stage was erected in the back yard. This intersection, because of the many cowboys who worked in nearby studios, was known as "Gower Gulch."

and the two of them strutted around like a pair of peacocks, proudly telling one and all, especially Keystone players, how much they were making. Sterling made a beeline for Charles Levi and Son, one of the foremost tailors in town, and ordered a half dozen suits at $90 each, three or four topcoats at $125 apiece, and as soon as he got them he wanted a couple of weeks off to go to New York City. When he got there, he took a suite of rooms at the Astor Hotel. Whenever he met anyone he knew, he took them up to his suite to proudly display his wardrobe. Lehrman spent his nights and money at Baron Long's Vernon Country Club flipping twenty-dollar bills to Mike Lyman and Whitey Clark, club entertainers, every time they stopped at his table to sing a song for him.

Sterling returned from New York in three weeks flat broke, while Lehrman was about in the same situation. Production of Sterling comedies continued to be a big success for a while, making it appear that my troubles were over, but toward the end of the year, the continued success had so affected both Sterling and Lehrman that it became impossible to get a day's work out of either. They would argue for hours at a time over how to play a scene as the crew stood around and waited. They came to hate each other so much that when Lehrman ordered Sterling to be on the set at nine in the morning ready to work, Sterling, who resented Lehrman's ordering him around, would show up at noon. Lehrman, to show his importance, would be gone when Sterling arrived. The following morning Sterling would be ready to go to work at nine but Lehrman wouldn't show up until noon. This nonsense went on until it got so that it took two weeks to make a five hundred-foot film, whereas Bob Thornby was knocking out one of our child comedies every week.

The feud between Sterling and Lehrman reached a point where I just had to fire Lehrman rather than Sterling since Sterling was the basis of my contract with the Universal company. This meant that I had to direct the next several Sterling comedies, each one of which became more aggravating than the previous one. Then, to top it off, Sterling became ill and sent a messenger in each week for his salary check. It was three weeks before somebody tipped me off as to what his "sickness" really was; Sterling had been spending his nights at Baron Long's night club whooping it up. One night I surprised him there in all his glory, putting it on high, wide, and handsome. I realized that I would also have to fire Sterling even though I had no idea what to do next. Then I remembered that I had thousands of feet of unused scenes and cutouts stored away in the vault from the many Sterling comedies we had made. One of our comedians, George Jeske, was about Sterling's age, size, and build, and was always imitating Sterling just for the fun of it. I made some test shots of him dressed in Ford Sterling's outfit of high hat and chin whiskers. Much to my relief, it was impossible to tell the difference between Sterling and him when he put on his act. Stories were concocted around the many scenes from the film in the vaults and we made use of Jeske in Sterling's place whenever we needed a key scene to smooth out the continuity. In this way we made Sterling comedies long after I had let him go for breach of contract. One of the comedies we made in this fashion was perhaps the best in the entire series. No one ever caught on to what we had done. At last we had no more film from the vault to work with so early in 1915 I disbanded the Sterling Film Company.

After Chaplin had gained some experience in moving pictures, I began to consider him as a comedian with promise. I knew he was not under contract and that he was earning one hundred and fifty dollars a week. *Tillie's Punctured Romance* had not yet been released, but I had seen it and was sure this picture would make him, so I offered him five hundred dollars per week, plus twenty-five percent of the profits. Charlie and his brother, Sydney, who was acting as his manager, accepted my offer, and I had Frank Graham draw up the contracts. They were never signed. Syd Chaplin was a smart cookie and no doubt figured that if I could make Charlie that kind of an offer, perhaps one of the larger companies would pay far more. Whether or not the news leaked out that Chaplin was not under contract, I don't know, but George K. Spoor of Essanay suddenly got into the picture and had his partner, Broncho Billy Anderson, come down from Niles, California, where he made his western pictures, to Hollywood with orders to sign Chaplin, which he did — right under my nose! Although the contract called for twelve hundred dollars a week, plus, I believe, one cent a foot of sold films, that contract proved to be a great bargain for Spoor. Charlie always claimed that I backed out of my offer. This is not true. Even after all the trouble I had with Lehrman and Sterling, I made something like seventy-five thousand dollars that year so I had ample finances to go through with the deal.

There is something more to be said about the phenomenal success of Charles Spencer Chaplin. His cleverness as a mime, his feeling for comedy that made it possible for him to be funny, sympathetic, or even dramatic, were assets he had always possessed. But they could easily have been lost, and he would have gone as unnoticed as so many had before him. What made the difference in Chaplin's case was that when he went with Essanay, they were wise enough to give him much more freedom and authority and the most important privilege — the right to edit his own pictures.

Charlie Chaplin was a fine comedian but that was only partly responsible for his success. He quickly learned to discard the old footage yardstick technique for cutting moving pictures, substituting instead delicate touches, such as a slight twist of the mouth, or a shrug of the shoulder that served as a guide to cutting the action precisely. The entire comedy industry soon copied his cutting technique, but to this day I have never heard anyone mention it or give him credit.

About a week before I was to leave for New York in April, 1915, to form the Quality Pictures Corporation with Joe Engel and Richard Roland, I had a letter from Arthur Miller telling me that he had left Pathé and had signed a contract to go to Detroit with an outfit I had never heard of, the Esperanto Film Company. Arthur was enthusiastic about his new job. At that time there were a lot of fly-by-night outfits around with stock-selling rackets, or some angel would put up money to make one picture just to satisfy his number one girl friend. I certainly hoped that Arthur hadn't been taken in by one of those deals.

In New York Joe Engel, Richard Roland, and I incorporated Quality Pictures Corporation for twenty-five thousand dollars, each of us putting up one-third of the money, with the stock split three ways. I was named president, Roland became vice-president, and Engel the secretary-treasurer of Quality. Our pictures were to be dramatic features and were to be released through Metro, recently set up by Roland, who was president, and Engel, Metro's vice-president.

When I learned that Francis X. Bushman, Essanay's heart-throb, was in New York and available, I went after him. Others had the same idea in mind. On the last day he planned to be in the city, Bushman finally consented to talk with me a couple of hours before his train, the Twentieth Century, was due to pull out for Chicago. I remember very well watching Carl Laemmle as he talked to him like a Dutch uncle in the lobby of the hotel while I stood on the sidelines impatiently waiting and getting nowhere. Suddenly I decided the only way to be alone with Bushman so that I could present an offer was to get on the same train and go with him to Chicago, even if I had no luggage. As things turned out later, I wish I had missed the train.

Bushman, who was married and had five children, was idolized by women. He was a sculptor's model and had won "the most handsome man" contest sponsored by *Ladies World* magazine before he became an actor at the Essanay studio in Chicago. He was over six feet tall, with dark curly hair, and was a strikingly handsome, virile-looking man in his early thirties. Bushman always appeared as if he had stepped out of a fashion plate. The night following our arrival in Chicago, I signed him to a contract while he, Beverly Bayne, his leading lady at Essanay, William Aranson, his manager, and I were having dinner together at the College Inn, a night club in the Sherman Hotel. The contract was for two years; it called for him to star in a series of films for Quality Pictures at seven hundred and fifty dollars per week, plus a percentage of the profits. The pictures were to be made in my Hollywood studio, but Aranson explained that Bushman could not very well leave Chicago before paying off some of his debts. I gave him a personal check for ten thousand dollars as an advance against his share of the profits, which, in fact, guaranteed the validity of the contract. I thought I had him figured out and, true to my expectations, I'll be damned if he didn't plank down about half of the advance on a special maroon-colored Marmon automobile the very next day.

After I had straightened out all the details with Bushman's manager, Aranson, it was arranged that I would meet them in Chicago on May 15 and from there we would all go on to the Coast to start making Quality's first picture. I had made contingent arrangements with Harry Reichenbach, one of the best publicity men of the time, to become head of that department if I were able to sign Bushman. This task accomplished, I wired Reichenbach to the effect that everything was OK, that I had signed Bushman, and that he should get busy.

With everything settled and nothing else of any great pressure to attend to, I decided to stop off in Detroit en route to New York so that I could have a visit with Arthur Miller. When I reached him by telephone at the Esperanto studio, he was surprised to hear my voice. I told him I'd like to stop off and pay him a visit, since it was only an overnight trip from Chicago. He was agreeable so the next morning the cab driver helped me to find the Esperanto studio in a loft building on Grashet Avenue where they occupied the second floor. Arthur was waiting. He appeared somewhat nervous. The lad I remembered had changed considerably in the six years since I had last seen him. Now twenty years old, Arthur had matured a great deal. The Esperanto studio was still in the getting ready period. General Electric in Detroit had supplied lights free of charge for the studio as an experiment, and row upon row of 1,000 watt incandescent light globes, with glass of a bluish tint, had been installed in the hope they would prove satisfactory as studio lights for photographing. The lights were arranged in banks of three rows of six globes, one above the other. On the bottom of each frame, which held eighteen globes, were casters to make it possible to move them around the floor. Electricians were busy doing the necessary work, and for my benefit Arthur had them light one of the cluster of lights. I immediately realized that the tremendous heat thus generated would make the idea impractical. I didn't think Arthur was aware of this nor did I offer my opinion. I thought it would be better if he made the discovery for himself.

Esperanto's laboratory had a nicely equipped rack and tank system, and a couple of Simplex step-printers. We spent the whole day together and then I took the New York Central's "Wolverine," to New York, arriving there the next morning. My partners were jubilant over my success in acquiring Bushman, and Harry Reichenbach started at once to turn out stories publicizing Francis X. Bushman as the "Woman's Choice."

We arrived in Chicago a few days before May 15, the agreed time to pick up Bushman and leave for the West Coast. Harry Reichenbach, with his sharp nose for publicity angles, had a canvas strip made up the length of the baggage car with high lettering reading, "Francis X. Bushman . . . Star . . . of Quality

Pictures Corporation," and about an hour or so before the train was due to leave, he attached the strip to our private baggage car that carried Bushman's Marmon automobile, his rare birds, Great Dane dogs, and a couple of saddle horses. It sure attracted a lot of attention before and as we pulled out of the station bound for Los Angeles.

Among those I signed shortly after I arrived in Hollywood to make the Bushman pictures were Marguerite Snow of the *Million Dollar Mystery* fame as leading lady, Lester Cuneo, the heavy who had played opposite Bushman at Essanay, William Clifford, a supporting actor, and William Alder as my cameraman. Harry Reichenbach took on Efe Asher as publicity assistant.

The Second in Command, our first picture, was taken from a play that had starred the great actor John Drew. It was a British war story that just suited Bushman's type and allowed him to display his best qualities while dressed in the tailor-made British officer uniforms he wore in the picture.

Besides being an outstanding picture, *The Second in Command* contained a technical innovation. William Alder, the cameraman, was an inventive sort of man. In the early twenties he worked on and thought he might be successful in making and projecting stereoscopic pictures without the aid of anything worn over the eyes to allow each eye to see its individual picture. Of course it never materialized. While going over the script for our first picture, it seemed to us that we would have to come up with something new in production to match the class of our new star, Bushman. We decided to plan the action of some scenes to make it possible to follow the actors, especially Bushman, and to move into a close-up without making a cut. We certainly weren't thinking of anything as elaborate as we wound up with. We drew a rough sketch of a platform large enough to set the tripod on with the camera and cameraman that could be moved on four wheels. When it was constructed, we found we would have to enlarge it to accommodate a second person. As the platform was pushed forward, it became difficult for Alder to crank the camera, watch the actors to judge distance as the platform moved, and follow the focus all at the same time. And so it went. We were continually taking the rolling platform in to our small carpenter shop and having it altered to meet our needs as they became more and more complex. By the time *The Second in Command* was finished, the platform was an underslung affair that hung from the axles and rode about four inches from the floor. We began calling the moving camera "trucking shots" and the platform a "truck." The axles had been prepared to allow the platform to move in a slight curve.

Of course the scenes had to be planned precisely in order to coordinate the movement of the truck with the panning and tilting of the camera, and it was most important that the actors cooperate for they were part of the entire planned movement of the scene. Bushman had never been disciplined to this kind of coordinated movement before and he gave us a little trouble. Making a film this way took more time but after looking at the rushes, we thought it worthwhile. Besides, it added that something extra to the production of the picture.

In 1956, thirty years after *The Second in Command* was made, I received a letter from James Card of the George Eastman House in Rochester, New York (a museum of early moving pictures and still photography) inquiring as to how these moving shots were accomplished at that time. I did my best to explain the procedure in detail, for it was gratifying to know that our efforts had merit.

The late Kenneth Macgowan in his book *Behind the Screen* says:

> Lately I have seen an American film of 1915, *The Second in Command*, in which the camera moved as skillfully as in any picture today. It rolled in as smoothly and unobtrusively from a group shot to the two principals, from a medium shot to a close-up. The camera caught a man outside a door, then cut to the room inside, showed his face as the door opened, pulled back as he entered, and finally gave us a full shot when he joined the group within. More remarkable, perhaps, the camera followed the hero and heroine as they moved about in a dance scene. Discovered by James Card of the George Eastman House of Rochester, this picture seems a mysterious sort of a relic—a small masterpiece of movement forgotten for more than forty years.

Mr. Macgowan goes on to say that a trade paper of 1915 states that Mr. Alder was the owner of perhaps the most elaborate laboratory in America. I believe they meant Joe Aller, who was the owner of such a laboratory for many years. The error could easily have occurred through the similarity in names.

The film processing of *The Second in Command* was done in our own Quality Pictures laboratory which I later sold. It became the Horsley laboratory. The man who was responsible for Quality's processing was John Seitz who became one of the best cameramen in the business. He will be remembered particularly for his photography of *The Four Horsemen of the Apocalypse*, as well as *Sunset Boulevard* and many other achievements.

The Second in Command was previewed in one of the better-class houses in Chicago, Bushman's hometown, with Bushman making a personal appearance. Since the preview took place in the morning, nearly ninety percent of the audience consisted of women who aahed, oohed, and sighed throughout the picture and swarmed around Bushman when the screening ended, buzzing like bees.

The picture, plus Reichenbach's eye-catching publicity campaign, put Bushman over with a bang. During the Panama Pacific World's Fair in San Francisco late that summer, Reichenbach pulled a bold stunt that put Bushman's picture on the front pages of all the papers in San Francisco and Oakland as well as other nearby towns. Harry had arranged to have Bushman make a personal appearance at the fair grounds, as well as act in several movie scenes which I directed. On the day before the stunt was planned for the cocktail hour, the entire company, consisting of Bushman, Marguerite Snow, Lester Cuneo, Efe Asher, Bill Alder, Harry Reichenbach, and I arrived at the St. Francis Hotel. Back in those days the cocktail hour at that hotel was something to see, and during the height of it a smartly dressed, beautiful woman in black, bedecked with sparkling jewels, pushed her way through the crowded lobby toward the hotel desk. From under her wrap, she produced a parcel the size of a cigar box which she shoved toward the desk clerk, saying breathlessly, "See that Francis X. Bushman gets this right away," and vanished. A ticking sound caused the clerk to beckon to a nearby house detective who put the parcel to his ear and then held it at arm's length as he gingerly marched toward the elevator, talking loudly about a damn bomb and Bushman. "Top floor," he barked to the elevator boy, "and make it fast."

Harry Reichenbach, of course, had the reporters lined up at the bar bending their elbows when the excitement of a bomb having been delivered to Bushman reached them. With the reporters hot on his heels, Harry made a beeline for the top floor and men's rest room where the detective was engaged in soaking the bomb in a basin of water. Meanwhile Asher came to where I was planted in the cocktail lounge and in a voice loud enough to be heard in China, gave me a quick rundown on what had happened. We were both puffing away on big cigars as we barged into the room where the detective was soaking the bomb. When he saw us, he almost blew his top. "Get outter here with those cigars," he yelled. "You wanna get us all killed?"

With the exception of the *Call-Bulletin*, whose reporters recognized a plant, the morning papers went to town with the story of a mysterious woman in black who had tried to bomb Bushman. When we arrived at the fairgrounds that afternoon, the place was overflowing with women, young and old, who had flocked there in droves just to see the virile and handsome Bushman. To protect him from any possible harm, Harry, always alert to the publicity angle, talked the officials of the fair into providing a guard. Flanked by a couple of dozen uniformed fairgrounds police, we paraded Bushman in all his glory through the jam-packed grounds, said to be the largest crowd the fair attracted during its run. As far as I know, the only ones in on the bomb stunt aside from Harry, Asher, and me, was Harry's wife, the mysterious beauty in black, and perhaps the hotel detective, although I never did find out for sure.

While shooting his third picture, Bushman became rather hard to handle, as he wanted Beverly Bayne, who had been his leading lady at Essanay, to join him. Miss Bayne arrived there in time to play opposite him in *Pennington's Choice,* a story taken from a magazine that we shot in the Big Bear Lake country. My good friend, Jim Jeffries, who happened to be up there on a hunting trip, agreed to do several boxing scenes with Bushman. From this picture on, Beverly Bayne was Bushman's leading lady. Eventually they were married after Bushman and his first wife were divorced.

Bushman's next picture, *Rosemary,* like *The Second in Command,* had been a stage play starring John Drew and it was a beautiful love story. I had the scripts and sets all ready to start shooting when Bushman, even though he had approved buying the play, suddenly decided that the part was not for him. He didn't like this, that, or Hollywood, and, to top it all, he wanted to make his pictures in New York. In a way, I liked Bushman, and he seemed to like me, but he was getting too temperamental for me to lose any sleep over, so I arranged to send him to my partners in New York to worry about. We already had spent considerable money getting ready to do *Rosemary,* so I produced it with Marguerite Snow, William Clifford, Lester Cuneo, and Frank Bacon, who had written a play, *Lightnin',* that had a two-year Broadway run. William Bowman did a fine job of directing the picture and with good performances from the actors, *Rosemary* proved a box office success, even without Bushman.

One of the pictures Quality made was *A Corner In Cotton,* with an original story by Anita Loos, author of *Gentlemen Prefer Blondes.* The picture had the same cast as *Rosemary,* plus Frank Bacon's son, Lloyd, who was the leading man. Lloyd later became a successful director.

Al and Charles Christie had left the Horsley company (Nestor) to organize the Christie Film Company and were looking for a studio. They wanted to buy mine since it was idle at the time. I didn't particularly want to sell, but when they raised their offer to twenty-two thousand dollars, I just couldn't turn down a quick profit of eleven thousand dollars on an investment of two thousand dollars, especially after having used the studio for about a year. If I had held that corner of Sunset and Gower where the Columbia Broadcasting building stands today, it's hard telling what I could ask for it.

Chapter 11

WORKING FOR GEORGE FITZMAURICE

BOUT A MONTH AFTER Fred Balshofer's visit to me at the Esperanto studio in Detroit, I learned that the picture we were to make, starring Norman Hackett, already had been started by the previous company. It was they who had built the laboratory and studio but had not yet had the lighting equipment installed. Thousands of feet of film had been photographed in the mountains showing Norman Hackett, who was an exceptionally good-looking young man, posed with one foot resting on a rock, as he smoked a pipe and surveyed the beautiful surrounding mountain country. In all of the film there was no one but him, so there wasn't anything to provide a clue as to what the story was to be or what the picture was all about. We spent weeks sorting the thousands of feet of film of Norman Hackett and then the whole idea of starring him in a picture was abandoned.

The incandescent blue-tinted electric globes furnished by the General Electric Company didn't work out for two reasons. One was that it took too many globes to get enough exposure as we used orthochromatic negative which didn't have the high exposure speed ratings of today's panchromatic negative. The second great disadvantage was the tremendous heat reflected by the globes. We finally changed over to Cooper-Hewitt and arc lights. Back lighting was beginning to be used more and more in lighting interiors, and the 60 amp. spot, made by the Kliegl Light Company, became an integral part of the lighting equipment for those cameramen who kept abreast of the rapid advancements being made in the quality of photography. The day was nearing when cinematography would be recognized as an art in its own right. Early in 1915 I received a letter from the Cinema Camera Club in New York of which I was a member, telling me that the studios were now giving cameramen screen credit, along with the directors and actors. This meant, naturally, that I would receive screen credit on any pictures produced by the Esperanto company.

When I arrived in Detroit to join the Esperanto company, I enrolled in Giuseppe Florence's art class in order to study and learn the fundamentals of composition and related subjects for I had not forgotten the importance Fred Balshofer had placed on the composition of a picture when he was a cameraman. The art school had five night sessions a week.

Our first picture was called *Doll House Baby*, a two-reeler directed by Cora Adams. As I recall, it wasn't until around the end of the year that the picture was sold. After that Louis Mill chose to make a one-reel comedy with Ralph Worsley, a rather good comedian who was playing at the Avenue Theater with a stock company. After we cut the picture, Mill took it to show to the Essanay company in Chicago. He returned with a contract to make a series of one-reel comedies. With the deal came a man whom I first understood to be a writer, but before we started the series, he seemed to have a lot to say about all phases of the production.

My first instructions were that the faces of the actors must be white and the sets fully lit with no shadows. The "writer" was around all the time when we were shooting our first comedy of the series for Essanay, constantly reminding me that comedy couldn't be played in the dark. He said it over and over, as if to make it perfectly clear that he was a genius. The comedies we made didn't amount to much as far as the photography was concerned; it was merely a matter of setting them up, photographing them quickly, and then knocking down the sets. They presented no opportunity or no challenge for a cameraman and my only satisfaction was the salary. My contract ran out in March and, as they didn't mention it, neither did I.

In the early part of May, out of the blue, a wire arrived

from Louis Gasnier asking if I were available. Pathé had stopped producing, but the Astra Film Company, of which Gasnier was the president, was going to make pictures to be released by Pathé. It took me only two days to clear out of Detroit. Essanay sent a cameraman over to fill my job.

Returning to the Pathé studio in Jersey City Heights was like coming home. Many of the same people were still there in the same jobs they had when I left. I was happy to sign a one-year contract with the Astra Film Company and was assigned to George Fitzmaurice, the director. "Fitz," as most people called him, had already made his first picture for the Astra company, a film called *Via Wireless*. He wasn't planning to start another for a month, so I photographed a one-reel comedy, *Toot, The Tailor*, directed by E. Mason Hopper.

The Fitzmaurice company worked as a sort of separate unit and made one picture after another without much time in between. Ouida Bergere, then Mrs. Fitzmaurice, was writing

Florence Reed
in *At Bay*.

screen adaptations from A. H. Wood's stage successes, and each picture featured some Broadway star. *At Bay,* the first picture I photographed for Fitzmaurice, starred Florence Reed. It was a five- or six-reel feature, and the interiors were photographed with mixed Cooper-Hewitt, arc and daylight, and it often took considerable time to achieve the desired lighting. To my delight, I found that Fitzmaurice was as interested in having quality photography as I, and he was very patient and understanding when problems sometimes arose. He was well educated in art and made many helpful suggestions. He also designed and laid out his own sets. I am sure there must have been art directors even then, but all that I remember are men who came from the carpenter shop. There was a group referred to as "outside" men whose job it was to secure and rent the furniture and dressing for the sets. When the picture was finished, it was my job to wind the scenes on reels, one after another, in sequence and continuity, ready for Fitzmaurice to do the cutting, known as "editing" today.

As the picture progressed, we numbered the scenes in the following fashion: the first scene photographed, regardless of the scene number in the script, was marked number one; the second number two; the third number three; and so on. The camera boy carried a slate, some white chalk, and a small book to keep the record. The number on the slate began with number one and went on up in sequence, and alongside the slate number in the book was the scene number in the script, with a short written description of the shot. Extra shots in the same scene were followed by "A," "B," and "C," and so forth. While Fitzmaurice cut the picture I helped and then photographed the main, sub-, and spoken titles. There were no previews at theaters but sometimes there would be a special screening for the crew and a few invited guests.

Although our film was processed by the rack and tank system, the Pathé News Weekly part of the laboratory had begun processing their film by machine early in 1916. The negative of the one-thousand-foot weekly reel was edited, spliced, and printed on one roll. The roll of positive film was fed into the machine, developed, fixed, and washed, then dried as the film traveled up and down, over and under a series of spools in a glass cabinet, and then wound itself on a reel at the end of its journey. To my knowledge this was the earliest film processing machine ever built.

The first four pictures I photographed for Fitzmaurice were named *At Bay, New York, Fifth Avenue,* and *Big Jim Garrity.* Often, to add a little class to the picture, when we went on location to some huge estate we would take along a small matching section of an interior set that included a window or a door. When we found a suitable vantage point on the lawn, we set up our section that showed the beautiful view through the open window. The plan was to have one member of the cast make an exit from the set on the stage, enter our section and play a bit of business in front of the open window and then exit. Of course, he then would reenter the set on the stage in the studio. A section of the door was used in the same manner for entrances and exits, and it showed the exterior while the door was open. With the advent in the early thirties of rear projection all this was simplified.

Eighty amp. spotlights had appeared on the scene and their use brought about a noticeable increase in light effect photog-

Part of a set taken on location to capture exterior through window. Today this is easily done by background projection, sometimes called "process."

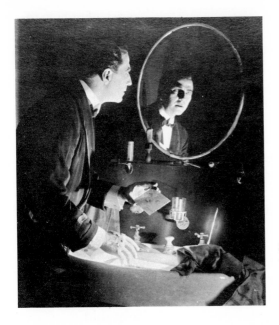

Scene from *At Bay*
with Charles Waldron.

raphy. Flat lighting gave way to modeling with highlight and shadow, and at this point I believe cinematography began its development toward finally being recognized as one of the arts.

All fades, lap dissolves, montages, and double exposures were made in the camera by the cameraman as part of his daily routine. Most cameramen had a Veeder counter added to their camera, and when they made double exposures, the frame at the aperture was marked and the counter set at zero. The cameraman was thus enabled to record not only the footage but also the number of frames that passed the aperture. If the camera was not equipped with a counter, the cameraman had to count the crank turns mentally.

To make a simple lap dissolve, the cameraman would fade out when the desired point in the scene was reached, usually in about three feet. With the shutter closed, he then cranked the camera backwards, reversing the film for the length of the fade. He then cranked forward while fading in, double exposing the film, thereby creating a lap dissolve. On cameras that did not have a dissolving shutter, the cameraman had the iris in the lens altered so that it could close completely; then he could make the fade-out and in with the iris. In cases of a lap dissolve where a fade-out was made and the scene it was to overlap into was to be made at a later date, the cameraman marked the frame of the aperture on the emulsion side of the film. He could then line the same frame at the aperture when threading the camera to make the second exposure another time. He made notes on a sheet of paper of the number of feet registered on the counter, or the number of crank turns, when he started the fade-out. In the darkroom he rewound the film, putting the aperture markings at the beginning of the roll. His written notes, together with the film, were sealed in a can for future use. When the time came, the camera was threaded, making sure that the marks were properly registered at the aperture and, with the shutter closed, the film was cranked through the camera until the counter registered the footage number corresponding with his notes. The action started simultaneously. As he cranked, he faded-in, completing the lap dissolve. The exacting cameraman always shot a test of the scenes he had photographed earlier and another before he shot the second exposure so that the scene he faded into would have the same density negative as the scene he faded from. This made a smooth lap dissolve without the necessity of a light change in printing. Rewinding film and holding it to shoot and complete at a later time was standard procedure in all double exposure trick shots.

In the real early days laboratory work was just as important to the cameraman as his work with the camera because the combination of both equaled photography. Many cameramen accomplished trick photography partly in the camera and partly in the step-printer in the laboratory. For example, to photograph the interior of a nickelodeon showing a picture on the screen and the audience in subdued lighting watching that picture, the set, with a white movie screen, was shot. The developed negative turned the white screen black and acted as a matte when the positive was being printed, and protected that portion of the picture from exposure. A suitable matte was then placed in the aperture of the step-printer to cover all but that portion representing the movie screen. By marking the frame-line for the second exposure, any chosen negative could be printed to represent the movie being shown on the screen. A fade-in or out or dissolve were often made on a step-printer, but the quality suffered greatly in those days and therefore was avoided whenever possible. Laboratory work in itself became a specialty, and gradually the cameraman came to depend entirely on those technicians for the processing of film. However, as late as 1925, cameramen were making their fades and laps in the camera. The establishment of optical rooms meant a great saving in time for the company shooting on the set, as well as the production of special effects unheard of before, perfectly acceptable in quality.

Matte shots were made with painted cardboard cutouts. This was a joint effort between the scenic department and the cameraman. The matching or blending edge of the matte had to be shaved down as thin as possible to prevent photographing the thickness or a reflection from it. Otherwise the shot was ruined. Matte shots were photographed on bright, sunshiny days so that the lens could be stopped down to the smallest opening in order to carry the focus from the matte that was placed about ten feet from the camera to the distant scenery, perhaps infinity. In the early twenties, the idea of painting the matte on a piece of glass and lighting it with artificial light greatly improved this type of photography which was called a "glass" shot from then on.

Our next picture, *Arms and the Woman,* starred Mary Nash, who was doing a play on Broadway at the time. There were three matinees each week, making it impractical for Miss Nash to travel to Jersey City Heights and back to New York the same day for her matinee performance. It was therefore decided to rent a studio in New York to make the picture. The studio chosen was located on West 57th Street, between Seventh and Eighth Avenues. It was a red brick church that had been transformed into a studio, only a short drive from the theater where Miss Nash was playing. The only lighting equipment in that studio consisted of banks of Cooper-Hewitt tubes, so we rented some broadside arcs and spotlights.

Fitzmaurice had hired Anton Grot as his art director. Grot was the first art director that I had the opportunity of working with who hadn't come up through the ranks from the construction department. Anton Grot was a gifted and talented artist who made beautiful charcoal drawings, approximately 11″x14″, of the set before it was constructed. All his compositions showed a full shot of each set, with all the delicate tones and shadings that suggested ideas for lighting and, in general, were of great help to me as cameraman. This new experience gave me an opportunity to consult and suggest breaks in the set to make it convenient for lighting and, in a practical sense, afforded me the opportunity to continue studying composition, with instruction from Anton.

The amazing thing about Anton's drawings was the application of a mechanical system he had worked out. The set, when constructed, duplicated his drawings in camera angle as well as showing sizes of objects in their proper relative proportions when photographed with a 40mm. lens. For his own use, he had made what he referred to as a "diminishing chart." This chart was worked out by using several lengths of 2′x4′ with a black line to mark each foot. Placed upright on end, beginning at six feet from the camera, they were spaced at one-foot intervals, increasing the distance to about one hundred feet. They were placed so that one would clear the other, and when viewed through the camera, all the 2′x4′ were visible from the bottom to the top of the camera aperture, with the one-foot spaces diminishing in increasing distance from the camera. From one frame of the film photographed, Anton had an enlargement made on 11″x14″ bromide paper, over which he placed a clear piece of celluloid. He then etched a chart which gave him the proportion that a foot or yard diminished at any distance from the camera when a 40mm. lens was used. By measuring the distances from the floor plan of the set and using his diminishing chart as an overlay while making his drawings, they would match exactly when the camera was set on the long shot. This is a far cry from some of the production design boys of later years whose drawings, supplied to the producer and directors, had no relation whatsoever to the pro-

portions of the camera aperture or to the sizes of objects as
they diminished in comparison to any lens. These were merely
pretty pictures that could not be duplicated by the camera
but did look nice as decorations on the walls of the producer's
home or office.

Often Anton Grot and I would have dinner together at a
very special restaurant where he was a long-standing customer.
Called Hendricks, it was located on the north side of 56th Street,
halfway between the rear entrance to the Great Northern Hotel and Sixth Avenue. Like many places on the side streets of
New York, it was in a brownstone residence that had been
converted into a restaurant. The restaurants specialized in
some special variety of food, French, Hungarian, or Spanish,
but Hendricks served only German food. The entrance from
the street to the lower floor, where the kitchen was located,
was three steps below the sidewalk level. A flight of brownstone steps led from the sidewalk up to the first floor, which
was furnished with tables and chairs, as was the floor above,
to accommodate the customers. There were a number of illus-
trators, portrait painters, and commercial artists, whose studios
were on 57th Street, as well as dealers in antiques, who gathered at the restaurant. Several art students who had part-time
jobs in the neighborhood were frequent customers. One of

An example of
Anton Grot's
pictures drawn
to scale.

these was William Menzies, to whom Anton introduced me. Another time I met the celebrated illustrator, Penrhyn Stanlaws, whose portraits of beautiful girls executed in pastel crayon were appearing regularly on the cover of the *American Magazine,* a popular Hearst publication of the era. On several occasions, Stanlaws questioned me about the opportunities and production methods of the movie business.

After we completed *Arms and the Woman,* we moved back to the Pathé studio in Jersey City Heights. In rapid succession, we made *Romantic Journey, The Iron Heart, The Recoil, The Mark of Cain,* and *Sylvia of the Secret Service,* which starred Irene Castle and Antonio Moreno. Erich Von Stroheim was a sort of technical director for this picture. Von had considerable knowledge of German militarism, or at least everyone thought he had. The plot of *Sylvia of the Secret Service* had something to do with the Germans blowing up an ammunition dump, and Von went to New York to research the names of the different explosives to be painted on cases stored at such a place. I don't believe that anyone ever saw Von Stroheim when he was not dressed other than as a dapper gentleman, with a rather short clipped haircut, Prussian style. These were the war years, and between his appearance and the sort of questions he was asking, it was no time at all before he was in the clink. The studio, of course, immediately went to his rescue and he was released. I am convinced, though, that the clever Von Stroheim pulled the whole thing off for its publicity value.

My contract with the Astra Film Company had expired and, as all the pictures I had photographed for them had been directed by Fitzmaurice, he proposed that I sign a personal contract with him. Gasnier had no objection so we went ahead. On his personal stationery Fitz wrote, "I agree to employ Arthur Miller as a cameraman for a period of one year and to pay him $75 per week as salary," which I signed and dated. Each year for the next eight years this process was repeated. During that period we never had a contract dispute, simply because there was nothing in the contract to dispute. Now when lawyers finish drawing up a cameraman's contract with its thirty pages of whereases and wherefores, there seems to be one continuing argument for its duration.

There were three or four other directors making pictures at this time at the Astra Film Company, but as far as I know Fitz was the only permanent one. All the better directors were striving for recognition and working to reach the heights of D. W. Griffith. Out of this desire, some directors gained further credit by having added to the main title something like "A George Fitzmaurice Production" as well as retaining the usual credit title, the last before the picture started, of "Directed by George Fitzmaurice." I use Fitzmaurice only as an example, not to imply that he began this practice, though he certainly was among the first.

After finishing *Sylvia of the Secret Service,* we moved from the Pathé studio in Jersey City Heights up to the Solax studio in Fort Lee on Lemoyne Avenue, a little bit west of what is now the George Washington Bridge Plaza. The Solax studio was practically the same as the Pathé studio; it had glass sides and top which meant mixing Cooper-Hewitt, arc, and daylight to photograph. Fitzmaurice took a well-deserved rest, while I photographed another picture also starring Irene Castle titled *Vengeance is Mine.* With Frank Crane as director, most of the picture was made in the Adirondack Mountains around Saranac Lake. We had returned to Fort Lee and were working in the studio when Miss Castle received the news that her husband, Vernon, who had joined the Royal Flying Corps, had been killed in an airplane accident while training in Texas. Both she and her husband had started breeding and training German shepherd dogs for war service. Miss Castle made me a present of one of the puppies which I loved for many years.

Our next picture, *The Naulahka,* starred Antonio Moreno and a sensational exotic dancer who called herself Doraldena. The first part of the story was laid in India, so Anton Grot designed a set representing the interior of a huge Hindu temple, with the foreground thirty feet deep where the action was to take place. The remaining depth of the set was built in what was termed "forced perspective." Although the actual depth of the entire set was no more than fifty or sixty feet, it appeared on the screen to extend for at least two hundred feet. When Fitzmaurice looked at a test of the set on the screen, he urged Grot to use the same method to build other sets in the picture. This

On location shooting *The Naulahka* on the Jersey side overlooking the Hudson River. George Fitzmaurice standing by the horse, with Antonio Moreno in the saddle.

gave Anton an opportunity to ask for an assistant. I knew he had Billy Menzies in mind, as they had often discussed the possibility when we met in Hendricks' restaurant. I did all I could to encourage the idea, not only because I liked Menzies, but also because Anton had been working long hours. Fitz agreed, and it wasn't long before Anton had taught Billy the trick of making drawings, using his dimension scale, which William Cameron Menzies used throughout his long and distinguished career as a production designer. The picture for which he is best remembered is Selznick's *Gone With the Wind,* produced in 1939.

After finishing *The Naulahka,* Louis Gasnier announced that the company was moving to California. There he was going to produce a serial *(Hands Up)* starring Ruth Roland and had hired James Horne to direct it. Fitzmaurice was scheduled to produce a series of feature pictures starring Fanny Ward.

Before we left the East, I did a few weeks' work on a new serial George Seitz had started to direct starring Pearl White and Antonio Moreno called *The House of Hate.*

House of Hate, a serial starring Pearl White and Antonio Moreno. *Left to right*, STANDING are Frank Redman, Jr., camera assistant, William Burt, assistant director, Harry Hardy, cameraman; KNEELING Buckley, stunt man, George B. Seitz, director, Arthur C. Miller, cameraman, unknown, and Pitch all-around grip-prop man who doubled in stunts. BOTTOM ROW: Pearl White, Helene Chadwick, Mrs. Arthur Miller, and George Seitz's mother, FOREGROUND: Antonio Moreno.

Chapter 12

THE YORKE FILM CORPORATION

OWEN MOORE, then Mary Pickford's husband, told me about a young and upcoming couple, May Allison and Harold Lockwood, who were making so-so pictures at the American Flying "A" studios in Santa Barbara, California. I went up to Santa Barbara to see Lockwood; he relayed my proposition to Miss Allison. After they had talked it over, they signed a contract for a series of pictures, Lockwood to be paid two hundred fifty dollars per week, while Miss Allison was to be paid two hundred dollars. Shooting was to begin on or about April 15, 1916.

The star, Harold Lockwood, a counterpart of Wallace Reid, was still in his early twenties. He was tall, manly, fair and handsome, while Miss Allison was a beautiful five-foot-two shapely blonde, a couple of years younger than Harold. Both were extremely likable. The day we signed the contracts, I left for New York to see if I could interest my partners in releasing the pictures through Metro. When I arrived, I found that they were having even more trouble than I had had keeping Bushman on the job. As a consequence, they were planning to unload him to Metro for stock which I, for some reason not now clear to me, did not want. I sold my interest for cash.

Since both Lockwood and Allison were practically unknown, I had to make their first picture at my own expense. The film turned out so well it enabled me to convince Dick Roland and Joe Engel that I had a couple of possible stars. It was a moonshine story that I both wrote and directed and was shot in and around Bat Cave in the heart of the Blue Ridge Mountains in North Carolina. Ray Smallwood, ace cameraman of the old 101 Bison days, photographed the film. Harold Lockwood and May Allison came east from Hollywood to do the picture, which cost nearly $16,000 to produce. Never will I forget the hard time we had convincing the suspicious local moonshiners that we were not Revenue men. In fact, it was not until Mr. Turner, owner of the Esmeralda Inn where we were staying, talked heart-to-heart with the moonshiners that they were convinced of the relative harmlessness of our activities. Authentic liquor stills, real moonshiners, and all of their paraphernalia added much to the realism of the picture. Ray's photography of the superb mountain country, added to the excellent performances of the cast, convinced Engel and Roland that it would be a good idea to set up a motion picture producing company with me. Each of us put up $8,333 to incorporate as the Yorke Film Corporation. I was named president, with Roland as vice-president, and Engel as secretary-treasurer. All of our pictures were released through Metro, who actually financed the films by paying the production costs, plus ten percent, on delivery of each negative.

Shortly after the establishment of the Yorke Film Corporation, Harold Lockwood, May Allison, and I went back to Hollywood to produce our pictures. For the purpose, I bought a studio on Gordon Street, just south of Sunset Boulevard, only a stone's throw from the one I had sold to the Christie brothers. These pictures soon became popular. We traveled to distant locations to photograph many of the films. Locations such as isolated snow-covered logging camps along the Dead River country in upper Maine and the logging camps in the big redwood country of Oregon made perfect backgrounds. We also took advantage of the tropical scenery in and around Palm Beach, Florida, as well as the colorful mountains.

Authentic locations played no small part in the success of these pictures. Among the titles were *Under Handicap, The Promise, Haunted Pajamas, Paradise Garden, Broadway Bill, The Square Deceiver, Lend Me Your Name, Pidgin Island, The Hidden Spring,* and *Man of Honor.* We went to a location along the rough and rocky seacoast off Monterey, California

Harold Lockwood with
Carmel Meyers in
Haunted Pajamas.

to make *Pidgin Island*. Harold, May, Tony Gaudio (my cameraman), and I nearly lost our lives when a huge wave suddenly
roared in from the ocean and swept over us. We were tossed
about like so many ninepins before we managed to grab and
hold onto a rocklike wall of the cove where the ocean had
washed us. After that wave receded, we were all so frightened,
we decided to call it a day.

My partners in New York were quick to notice May Allison's
increasing popularity and contracted with her to make a series
of films in which she was to star. I continued making the Lockwood pictures, using such talented actresses to play opposite
him as Carmel Meyers, Vera Sisson, Ann Little, Pauline Curley, Martha Mansfield, and Virginia Rappe, the ill-starred
exotic; stately, and beautiful ex-model whose death was the
basis of the many "Fatty" Arbuckle murder trials. Actors who
played prominent roles in Lockwood's pictures were Lester
Cuneo, William Clifford, Fred Heck, Francis Ford (who had
directed pictures for me at the Bison company), and Edward
Sedgwick. There were others, but Ford and Sedgwick eventually became outstanding directors. By 1918 Harold Lockwood had become one of the foremost stars when tragedy
struck. He died a victim of the flu epidemic that hit New York
that year, claiming hundreds of lives.

Scene from
Paradise Garden.
Second girl from the left
is Virginia Rappe,
with Harold Lockwood,
Vera Sisson, and
William Clifford.

On November 11, 1918, the day World War I ended, I had just completed cutting and titling a six-reel all-out anti-Kaiser picture. It starred Julian Eltinge with Virginia Rappe, William Clifford, and Fred Heck in the other principal roles. Rudolph Valentino had a supporting part at twenty-five dollars per day. Despite the fact that it was a well-made big picture, nobody wanted to show war pictures now that the conflict was over, so I lost nearly eighty thousand dollars on it.

About two and a half years later, I managed to retrieve almost half of my loss, as Valentino had become a big star by virtue of his performances in *The Four Horsemen* and *Blood and Sand.* I remembered that he had appeared in the war picture I had made in 1918, so I dug it out of the vault, spent around ten thousand dollars shooting additional scenes, stuck in all the cutouts of him that I could, and changed the main title. By using different spoken titles, it was possible to alter the picture from a serious one to a light comedy. I renamed it *The Isle of Love,* and publicized it as co-starring Valentino and Eltinge. Distribution rights were sold state by state—the so-called States Rights market. In its new dress, the picture was doing fine until the market became flooded with reissues of pictures in which Valentino appeared, no matter how small his part or how bad his acting was.

While I was in New York City in the spring of 1919, Harry Cohn and his brother, Jack, a couple of youngsters in the film business, wanted me to go in with them to form a company to make a series of comedies called *The Hall Room Boys,* based on a popular newspaper strip. I was to put up half of the money required, which amounted to only a few thousand dollars, so I agreed. When the time came to set up the company, the Cohns proposed to split the stock three ways, share and share alike. Inasmuch as they, together, were going to contribute only the same amount as I, it seemed to me that they were trying to pull a fast one, and I told them so. Anyway, I was preparing to make a series of westerns at my Hollywood studio for the States Rights market, so I called the deal off.

Harry Cohn had been in the music business, and then an exhibitor of roadshow films, and he was a quick and aggressive man in his late twenties. Jack had been in the advertising agency field, a laboratory man with Carl Laemmle's Imp Company, and an editor of the *Universal Newsreel.* Joe Brandt, who they talked into joining them after I backed out, was around Jack's age and also worked for Universal in the sales department. Together they formed the C.B.C. Pictures; Cohn, Brandt, and Cohn. Brandt was president, Harry vice-president, and Jack secretary-treasurer. After fooling around in New York for a while, they came to Hollywood where they rented part of my studio on Gordon Street, which they used for nearly a year, and made their *Hall Room Boys* comedy series with Lee Moran and Neely Edwards as stars. They operated under the name What Not Company, on a very thin bankroll, but were extremely successful and in approximately five years reorganized their C.B.C. company as Columbia Pictures Corporation. In 1932 Harry bought out Brandt's holdings and became president.

They really worked hard during those early days, with very little money, as well as in later years when Harry, as production head, ground out pictures on the coast, while Jack and Joe sold them. Jack and Joe alternated on sales trips from their hole-in-the-wall office in New York City. When they had the low-down on what type of pictures the exhibitors wanted, they sent the information on to Harry, who produced them. Cheap pictures they were, it is true, but the Cohns sold them and they forged ahead. In my opinion, they deserve much credit; Harry and Jack Cohn raised Columbia to top rank in the industry. Success such as the Cohns had, starting as they did with practically nothing but driving ambition, tireless effort, and, most important, the courage to compete against the well-established, are elements anyone in the business in those days admired.

To produce our upcoming western series, it was apparent that we needed a change in background in order to distinguish our pictures from the run-of-the-mill westerns that were being shot short distances from Hollywood. Many of these were completed in ten days and consequently were christened "quickies." My assistant and I traveled as far as Tucson, Arizona, on our search but the residents by now were picture-wise and thought this would bring them a bonanza and priced everything accordingly.

We found an ideal location near Julian, California, a small town about forty miles northeast of San Diego and about fifty miles from the Mexican border. It was a cattle ranch, belonging to Rodriquez Lopat, and was part of an old Spanish grant. The ranch was surrounded by rolling hills and canyons, reminiscent of the Santa Ynez Canyon where we made our 101 Bison pictures in the early days. Scattered about the ranch house were the stables, blacksmith shop, hay barns, and bunkhouses for the cowboys and work hands. Still standing were some of the old adobe brick buildings, reminders of the past.

There was plenty of room to house our company, consisting of Fred Church, the main character, who had been a foil for Broncho Billy Anderson for many years, Bud Osborne, Art Ortega, Jess McGaugh, and Julia Jones, our leading lady. The ranch had a vast assortment of equipment that we made use of in our western pictures. The boss gave the cowboys working on the ranch permission to play in our films, and they were delighted at the opportunity.

We started shooting our first picture in the summer of 1919, and after the exteriors of the first film were finished, we returned to our studio in Hollywood to make the interiors. After making five of these fast-riding gunplay pictures, they were so successful that I started thinking about selling the Hollywood studio and building one somewhere close to the ranch. We had completed the series of eight, all of which ran about five or six reels each, when I began to have trouble with my hearing. We were preparing to make a deal for another eight films but this new development delayed my plans. As my hearing grew worse, despite the best treatment available, friends gave me hope that nevertheless my trouble could be overcome. It is hard to explain my anxiety during this period. As I look back now, it seems to me that I was sure I was embarking on a new adventure that would outdo the success of the Bison company where it all started. I knew I was wiser now and had no partners to worry about, but the gradual loss of hearing seemed to put me out of contact or disassociated me from the pictures I was to make. Then, as now, one must be closely involved and in the middle of everything in order to produce a good picture. So I waited for my hearing to improve.

After sound came in, I was persuaded to make a series of Spanish-language pictures—the title was to be *The Lion Tamer*. The actors were to be supplied from a Spanish theater in downtown Los Angeles. After I had started the first five-reel picture, I knew the deal wasn't practical. There were many costly delays; for example, we waited for actors, most of whom were very temperamental. My assistant, the interpreter, and I, as well as the entire crew, had to wait for hours before we could get started each day, making the cost prohibitive. Although the first of the series was very well received, I lost money on it. More important, though, I realized it was impossible for me to work under these strained conditions, as I did not understand Spanish and was dependent upon an interpreter. Padding the walls of the sound stage, necessary for sound recording, made it difficult for me to hear anything. The complications became too great. Under the circumstances, I sold the contract for the remainder of the series.

I never actually did make up my mind to retire, but as the years passed, I realized that my picture-making days were over and a feeling of contentment replaced my disappointment. Knowing that I had a small part in widening the path of innovations leading to the wonderful world of motion pictures, makes me feel that I accomplished something worthwhile.

Chapter 13

FILMING MAE MURRAY, ELSIE FERGUSON
RICHARD BARTHELMESS, AND OTHERS

WHEN THE ASTRA COMPANY arrived in Los Angeles in June, 1918, they went directly to the Universal studios as previously arranged. There they occupied a small office building and one enclosed stage. The stage was equipped with twin broadside arc floor lamps, top light arc scoops, several 80 amp. spots, and Cooper-Hewitt floor banks used for filler light. Mixing of daylight for photographing interiors was becoming a thing of the past, and the glass panes in several studios that had been built to use daylight were now painted black. The sun arcs, really Sperry searchlights, had been promoted by Sperry in 1917 for use as studio lighting, and there were a few cameramen in Hollywood who used them. Later these searchlights proved to be ideal for shooting night exteriors. Although the Bell & Howell camera was used quite extensively in Hollywood at that time, I still used my Pathé, as did many other cameramen.

The climate in Southern California in 1918 was hard to believe unless actually experienced. The rainy season extended from about the middle of December to the middle of March, and most of the time the rain fell at night. The rest of the year the sun came up bright every morning. There was no such thing as a "weather permitting" call for extras the following day. During the rainy season there was some fog from the sea that extended inland for almost ten miles, but this usually burned off by noon. Smog was unheard of and nonexistent.

To my surprise, many directors and cameramen wore riding breeches and puttees, even when working on stages. Another noticeable difference was the lack of interest in anything in the community apart from the moving picture business. Everybody was in it, and everybody talked about it and nothing else. A few directors apparently assumed that they were the kings of their own little domains and were accepted as such by their subjects or "yes" men. This, however, was not the general practice. Each shooting company had its own musical combo, usually made up of a portable organ, a violin, and a base viol. It was the combo's job to play sideline music while the scenes were being photographed: happy songs for happy scenes and sad songs for sad scenes. In this select group, there always seemed to be a contest under way as to which director was entitled to the largest megaphone, and of far greater importance was the size of the letters painted on it that spelled out his name. Since these were silent pictures, constant vocal direction from the megaphone, mixed with the music, must have been a little disconcerting to the actors. One director was blessed with a strange status symbol in the form of a young man whose sole job it was to carry a stool around and whenever the director paused, place the stool ever so gently so that all the director had to do was to bend his knees to be seated. Nobody dared to imitate this maneuver so it remained that particular director's exclusive for many years.

Of course, the majority of directors needed none of this phony fanfare to make the outstanding pictures that are a part of motion picture history. The technical people, electricians, grips, and all the others concerned, left nothing to be desired. Working with the same equipment on the east and west coasts had standardized the efficiency of most of the crafts. Denver Harmon, one of Universal's gaffers, made an effort to acquaint me with most of the people on the lot, and his assistant or "best boy," Frank Murphy, was destined to perform a major part in changing the whole concept of silent motion pictures into talking pictures some ten years later.

The Profiteers starred Fanny Ward in the role of a nun.

Astra's first West Coast picture was called *Common Clay*, and it starred Fanny Ward. Her second for Astra was *The Profiteers*, followed by a war story. We were lucky enough to get Von Stroheim as our technical director for this one. He saw to it that all the German uniforms were correct and taught the soldiers how to goosestep. Stroheim was the busiest man in town then, as all the companies were making war pictures. After these three movies were completed, the Astra company moved over to Glendale to the studio where the Baby Marie Osborn pictures had been made. Fitzmaurice directed a few more features starring Fanny Ward and Lew Cody. A short while later the company went out of business due to neglect on the part of the management. Fitzmaurice decided to return to New York, but I had enjoyed the short while I had been in California and wanted to remain. We therefore agreed to call off the remaining period of our agreement. After everyone left, I felt somewhat alone in a strange place.

A few weeks later Dal Clawson, a cameraman I had never met, telephoned me and arranged a meeting at Jack Bloom's laboratory on Sunset Boulevard and Gardner Street. Clawson said that he had heard of my plans to stay in California and that he thought he could get me the job he was leaving, photographing Sessue Hayakawa, provided I asked for a hundred

and fifty dollars a week and continued to have the film processed at the laboratory of his friend, Jack Bloom. Since this
was agreeable to me, Clawson telephoned Hayakawa and made
an appointment for me to meet him that evening at his home
on the corner of Argyle Street and Franklin Avenue in Hollywood. Hayakawa and his charming wife treated me more like
a guest than a cameraman looking for a job. When Hayakawa
heard that I had been photographing Fanny Ward, he told me
that it was the picture he played in with her called *The Cheat*
that had been the turning point in his career, so he hired me
at one hundred fifty dollars a week without question.

The next morning when I reported to the Brunton studio
on Melrose Avenue, I was introduced to William Worthington,
Hayakawa's partner, who was also the director. The Brunton
studio was a huge lot where many different companies made
their pictures. (Today Paramount studio stands on the site of
the Brunton studio.) In addition to renting stage space, the
picture companies were also serviced by the departments that
were a part of the studio setup. The stages were enclosed and
the lighting equipment consisted of arc and Cooper-Hewitt
banks.

Because I hadn't met many cameramen in California, I joined
the Static Club, an organization of cameramen founded in 1913.
Its New York counterpart, founded a year later, was the Cinema
Camera Club. These clubs were partly social gathering-places,
but they also provided the chance for members to discuss problems of lighting, standardization of frame-line, and other matters concerned with the art of cinematography. Later both
organizations merged, and thus arose the American Society of
Cinematographers.

My second Hayakawa picture was almost completed when
a telegram came from Fitzmaurice asking me if I wanted to
join him at the Famous Players-Lasky Company. As soon as
the Hayakawa picture wound up, I was on my way back to
New York. The Famous Players studio had once been an indoor
riding academy and was not very large. The neighborhood was
already familiar to me as it was on the south side of 56th Street
between Sixth and Seventh Avenues, almost opposite the rear

entrance to the Great Northern Hotel. A little way down 56th
Street on the opposite side was Hendricks' German restaurant
where Anton Grot and I had spent so many pleasant hours.
Robert Haas, the head art director of the Lasky studio, was
well acquainted with Hendricks. Once again, luck was with me
for Haas assigned William Ihnen as art director to the Fitzmaurice company. Ihnen was a clever artist with an architec-
tural background, and one of the most cooperative men with
whom I ever have had the pleasure of working.

During the preparation of the first picture, *The Witness for
the Defense*, which was to star Elsie Ferguson, Bob Haas and I
visited the restaurant down the street frequently. On one of
these occasions, Penrhyn Stanlaws came over to talk with Haas,
whom he knew. When he recognized me, Stanlaws said he
had been wondering what had happened to Anton Grot and
me. I told him I had been in California, which provoked Stanlaws into asking many questions about picture-making there,
to the surprise of Haas. The result was that Haas invited Stanlaws to drop by the studio. The day he called, Bill Ihnen had
just completed the main set for the picture, a courtroom, which
was a duplicate of the real thing. The set was very impressive,
having been constructed of large mahogany panels, separated
by fluted pilasters with ornate bases and caps. Stanlaws mainly
was interested in knowing how Ihnen chose color tones to give
the appearance of mahogany and also how he could tell it would
photograph well. When Fitzmaurice came on the set, Bob Haas
naturally introduced him to Stanlaws. Fitz knew Stanlaws by
reputation, and they took an instant liking to one another. Fitz
dragged him off to his office to show him the sketches that
Ihnen had made of some other sets for the picture. From then
on, Stanlaws spent at least four days a week on the set while
we were shooting the picture. A few years later, Penhryn Stanlaws directed a picture for Famous Players. It starred Betty
Compson. It is my impression that Fitz arranged this. Although
it was a fine picture, unfortunately this was the only film Stanlaws ever directed.

The action of *The Witness for the Defense* took place mainly
indoors and, as stage space was limited, sometimes it was neces-

sary for three companies to shoot their sets, one beside the other. This eliminated the California idea of sideline music to get the actors in the mood, and the closeness of the shooting companies each making a different picture created a friendly respect among the directors so that when one was ready to shoot a scene, the others would stop rehearsing. The only way to insure privacy for scenes where the female star was scantily dressed or to play a scene that was intensely dramatic was to arrange a series of flats enclosing the open end of the set with a small space for entering and leaving. This became known as a "closed set," and a guard stood at the entrance. Once Adolph Zukor came to a closed set and the guard stopped him. In his soft voice, Zukor said, "But I am Mr. Zukor." "I don't care who you are," the guard, who had never heard of Zukor, answered. "This is a closed set." Zukor smiled, turned and left, returning with someone who the guard knew to have the authority to admit a visitor.

The quality of the production, plus what I thought was Fitzmaurice's best picture, *The Witness for the Defense,* placed him right among the top directors. Other directors at the 56th Street studio at that time were John Robertson, Hugh Ford, Chet Withey, and Jack Dillon, who had just arrived from the coast to make a picture with Justine Johnson.

Fitz's next picture was *The Avalanche,* with Elsie Ferguson playing the dual role of mother and daughter. An interesting photographic effect in this picture was in the scene where Miss Ferguson, as the daughter, was seated at a roulette table. She wore a Spanish shawl draped over her shoulders. As the mother, Miss Ferguson entered the scene and actually took hold of the daughter's hand and placed some money underneath it, watched her place a bet, and then made an exit. Split screen shots were common but to have one person playing two parts and touch each other was a novelty. To accomplish this, the matte was split on the shawl at the arm. Underneath the arm a cardboard sleeve, with a portion of the shawl over it, was fastened to the table. Taking the mother's side first, another girl's hand was slipped through the cardboard, and when the mother placed the money under the hand, a note was made of the camera crank turn as I counted aloud. The daughter reacted to the money placed under the hand as the turn of the crank came to the same number.

For *Society Exile*, Fitzmaurice's third picture, Bill Ihnen built a Venetian canal lined with old buildings on either side. The water in the "canal" was deep enough to float a few gondolas. Miss Ferguson and her leading man, William Carleton, played some romantic scenes on one of the balconies, all with a full moon in the sky.

Ouida Bergere (Mrs. Fitzmaurice) had now come into her own as a writer and for the next several years proved she had an unusual talent for writing for individual stars. She had the knack of interjecting scenes that allowed a particular individual to show himself at his best and thus greatly enhance his screen appeal. When Fitzmaurice finished *The Counterfeit*, also starring Miss Ferguson, Mae Murray arrived from California to make *On with the Dance* which he was to direct. There was

The shirt sleeve is fastened to the tree enabling a hand to be slipped through for the second exposure.

some delay in the script that Ouida Bergere was writing for Miss Murray, but Hugh Ford was ready to start *His House in Order* with Miss Ferguson. I was hopeful that I would get a little vacation, but instead Miss Ferguson arranged to have me photograph her picture until Fitz was ready to start with Miss Murray. *His House In Order* was finished with time to spare before Fitz started shooting *On With The Dance*.

As the title indicates, *On With The Dance* took place in one cafe after another. All the sets that Ihnen built were glamorized so that Mae Murray could dance her way through the picture, with a different light effect for each dance. For part of the picture, we used a new technique introduced by Billy Bitzer and Henry Sartov in D. W. Griffith's *Broken Blossoms,* called soft-focus photography. The soft-focus effects in *Broken Blossoms* were accomplished by photographing through a layer of gauze, and as the fad took over with all cameramen, special lenses were developed for the purpose. Among these was the Verito made by the Wollensack Company and another, the Graff Verable, allowed the amount of soft focus to be varied according to the taste of the individual cameraman. No doubt there were others, and some cameramen even designed their own soft focus lenses. The fad became so overdone that at times it was virtually impossible to identify the performer on the screen, but the feminine stars demanded it.

I started making the usual tests of Miss Murray, as was the custom if one had not photographed the star previously. These tests gave the cameraman the opportunity to learn which features to emphasize as well as those to avoid. Miss Murray issued a set of instructions as to where to place the lights for close-ups of her. As soon as it became evident that these instructions merely had been given to her, I politely ignored them and proceeded according to my own judgment. When she viewed the test, she approved of everything with the exception that there wasn't enough diffusion or soft focus, and it took several more tests to satisfy her. Of course, Miss Murray didn't understand that to cut from a medium shot of three people to a fuzzy close-up would look a little ridiculous. When the picture was shot, I limited the diffusion as much as I could.

On With the Dance,
with Mae Murray and
Holmes Herbert.

On With The Dance had less realistic photography than any
picture I photographed before or since. Nevertheless, with all
the trimmings and so-called glamor, plus the fuzzy soft-focus
close-ups, the picture was a big hit.

On With the Dance required so many sets that Bill Ihnen
had to construct some of them in the new studio that Famous
Players was building in Astoria, Long Island, even though it
wasn't quite completed. When it was finished in 1920, it certainly was a studio on a grand scale. The ground floor was one
huge stage that accommodated six or eight companies working
simultaneously. There were also two or three smaller stages in
the basement. The studio was fitted out with the latest in lighting equipment, and the laboratory was conveniently situated
across the street.

Ouida Bergere immediately got busy on a second script for
Miss Murray, while I started on another picture with Hugh
Ford titled *Lady Rose's Daughter*. This time Elsie Ferguson

played a triple role. Each character was of a different decade, starting in the early 1900's. *Lady Rose's Daughter* turned out to be a colorful picture because of the background and costuming, particularly as the gowns Miss Ferguson wore changed in style as the years progressed.

At that time, Famous Players-Lasky was the leader in the movie entertainment field, and there were so many companies working at the 56th Street studio that it became necessary to rent the Whitman Bennett studio up in Riverdale (near Yonkers) to make *Lady Rose's Daughter*. Every effort was being made to complete the studio in Astoria, and preparations already had been started for the next Mae Murray picture which was called *The Right To Love*. Bill Ihnen had been down in Florida building a South Sea island home for the film. Mae Murray was to play a sort of untamed young woman living with her father who made some homebrew which he sold to the natives while drinking more than his share of it. The leading man, David Powell, just happened to be cruising among the islands when he encountered the vivacious nature girl with whom he naturally fell in love.

Gus Crammer, the head electrician, was sorting over the electrical equipment before we moved to the studio in Long Island when he came across some camera cases that had been placed in his care. He showed them to me and asked why no other cameraman wanted to use the camera that had been bought for and used by Hal Young, a cameraman no longer with Famous Players-Lasky. I followed him down the ladder to the basement and there, in their original cases, were a camera, tripod, six four-hundred-foot magazines, and a full set of lenses—a complete Bell & Howell outfit. When I told Mr. Naulty, the studio manager, how useful the camera would be in Florida, he said he was glad to have it come to some use. From that day on I stopped using my Pathé.

Fitzmaurice, his wife Ouida Bergere, his assistant, Bob Schable, and I left for Florida about two weeks in advance of the actors. We lived in the only hotel that Miami then boasted, the Royal Palms, an ornate, large frame structure with gabled windows, five stories high and spread out over a considerable area. Several clusters of stately royal palm trees adorned the large lawn and the lower portion of the hotel was covered by a mass of purple-red bougainvillea blossoms.

The business part of Miami was on the north side of Flagler Street from the uncompleted MacCallister at the beach to about five blocks west. The sole restaurant was called the Wayside Inn. Across the beach road from the MacCallister, Flagler Street led onto a five-hundred-foot-long amusement pier constructed on pylons out over the water and on both sides were the usual carnival amusements, with fishing boats for hire moored on both sides.

A short boat ride took us to Bill Ihnen's island location where he had used driftwood and material he found there to build the house. The house, with a roof of dried palm thongs, was tucked into the shelter of a small cove. It looked as if it had been sleeping in the sun for years. Here and there a graceful sloping coconut palm tree danced in the breeze between the house and the beach, a distance of perhaps two hundred feet. The whole island was a cameraman's delight, with beautiful compositions wherever one looked. It was possible to shoot in any direction along the white, sandy beach, as there wasn't anything on the island other than the natural jungle growth. This doesn't sound much like Miami Beach, but that's how it looked in 1920.

It took us about five weeks to finish the Florida photography. Then we went back to New York to do the interiors in the 56th Street studio. Before we went to Florida, John Robertson was occupying the space next to us directing *Dr. Jekyll and Mr. Hyde*, starring John Barrymore. I happened to be watching his cameraman, Roy Overbaugh, the day he made the dissolve that transformed Dr. Jekyll into Mr. Hyde. Barrymore, in the role of the dapper Dr. Jekyll, finished mixing the dreadful concoction at his laboratory bench, then poured it into a glass. He moved to the foreground and sat down at his desk so that he could be seen full face. He raised the glass containing the magic potion, paused a moment, and then gulped the contents down. He stared straight ahead in wonderment for a few seconds while he waited for the potion to take effect. His face contorted

and his body began to stiffen. Finally, Barrymore lost his bal-
lance and fell from the chair to the floor behind the desk. He
had been instructed to fall in such a way that one hand would
remain on top of the desk. At this point, Roy Overbaugh made
a three-foot fade-out. The hand was carefully outlined where
it rested. Overbaugh reversed the film the length of the fade
back into the unexposed magazine and when Barrymore returned, now made up as Mr. Hyde, his gnarled, scrawny hand
was placed where the marks were on his desk. Overbaugh
started cranking and counting aloud. The overlap dissolve was
completed in the camera when the count reached six, Barrymore's cue to start raising his head from behind the desk, dis-
closing the ugly face of Mr. Hyde with his fanglike teeth and
straggly head of hair. By exerting a great deal of effort, Barrymore was able to raise himself back into the chair, where he
sat looking around for several seconds to give the audience an
opportunity to see his terrible face. Cutting back to a long shot,
Mr. Hyde was then shown as he snatched up his cane and
made his exit to prowl the dark streets and choose his next
victim.

Our next picture, *Idols of Clay* with Mae Murray, was made
at the new studio toward the end of 1920. After this picture
was completed, Miss Murray and Robert Leonard formed their
own company. It seems to me that their first production was
Peacock Alley. We made *Paying the Piper*, followed by *Experience*, both starring Richard Barthelmess who had become well
known for his work in *Broken Blossoms*. Despite all his success,
Richard Barthelmess had not become spoiled and was wonderful to work with. Nevertheless, compared with the Elsie Ferguson and Mae Murray pictures, *Experience* was not a hit
picture.

Peter Ibbetson, a play starring John and Lionel Barrymore,
was converted by Ouida Bergere into a movie script, and the
title was changed to *Forever*. Elsie Ferguson, Wally Reid,
George Fawcett, Eliot Dexter, and Montagu Love were in the
cast. *Forever* was one of those rare picture-making experiences
when every one seemed to be able to work in complete harmony. Everything about *Forever* fell into its proper relation-

Richard Barthelmess in *Experience*
facing the camera with
director George Fitzmaurice and
cameraman Arthur C. Miller.
After shooting toward house,
garden gate was moved
to capture a picturesque view
looking away from house.

Wallace Reid in *Forever*
from the play *Peter Ibbetson*,
now considered a classic
and his best
moving picture role.

ship and, while there was no apparent reason, everyone connected with the picture was entirely content. Preparation for the picture had not been any more diligent than usual nor was it a matter of enthusiasm, for I had started photographing other films with a lot more, but while I was watching the daily rushes some two weeks later, I realized that this was an extra special picture. The only comparison I can make is an individual way. There is an indefinable quality in the photographic images of some actors, while others lack this quality entirely. It has little to do with the beauty of a woman or the handsomeness of a man, for what "comes across" is invisible. Critics of that day and historians of today credit Miss Ferguson with the best performance of her entire film career, as well as applying the same superlatives to Wallace Reid and George Fawcett. *Forever* was said to be the best example of Fitzmaurice's direction, as well as Ouida Bergere's most successful film adaptation. As for myself, this was without a doubt the best photographic job of my entire career. Unfortunately, to the best of my knowledge, no print of *Forever* is now in existence. Only twice more in the next thirty years of photographing pictures did I experience this "everything's perfect" feeling: once was in 1941 while making *How Green Was My Valley*, directed by John Ford, and the second was in 1943 with *The Song of Bernadette* under Henry King's direction.

The portrait gallery and still picture laboratory at the Famous Players-Lasky Long Island studio were quite elaborate and I spent a lot of my spare time there. The boss of the department, Bill Lyman, became a good friend, and so did his portrait operator, Ernest Bachrach. One morning Lyman came to the set where we were working to tell me that a studio executive had sent a visitor to his department in seach of information, and he thought I could answer the questions. Lyman introduced me to the visitor who accompanied him as "Mr. Whitman" and said he was the brother of the then governor of the state of New York. It was almost noontime so Mr. Whitman suggested that we join him for lunch and discuss his problem. At lunch he confessed that he had become involved in something that he didn't know much about and was trying to

get some information on the subject. Whitman began by saying
that Tex Rickard, the famous prizefight promoter, had given
him the contract to arrange for photographing the coming
heavyweight championship fight between Jack Dempsey and
Georges Carpentier. This was about the middle of May and
the fight was scheduled to take place at Boyles Thirty Acres in
New Jersey on the afternoon of July 2, 1921. With a self-satis-
fied smile, he told us that he had been favored with the contract because his brother, the governor, had interceded in behalf of Tex Rickard and obtained assurances from the Attorney
General of the United States, Harry Daugherty, that if it were
possible to transform the fighters in the film to animated cartoons, leaving the remainder of the film as photographed, the
fight pictures would be permitted to be transported lawfully
from one state to another. I told him that this would present
no problems as Earl Hurd was making a weekly release of a
cartoon picture called *Johnnie Out of the Ink Well* that contained the very thing he was seeking. Each reel began by showing Hurd drawing Johnnie on a piece of paper, and when it
was finished, little Johnnie walked off the paper, up Hurd's arm,
and whispered in his ear, thus combining live action with a
cartoon. This seemed to please Mr. Whitman. He asked if it
would be possible to arrange a meeting at his apartment on
Riverside Drive. He also suggested that if Mr. Hurd was interested, something might be worked out whereby we all could
profit.

The suggested meeting took place in a few days, with Bill
Lyman, Hurd, and I among those present. We were introduced
by Mr. Whitman to his two sons, then in their middle twenties,
and to a friend of Whitman's named Wells. We talked for
about two hours, explaining fully the complete process from
photographing the fight to the finished product, with the fighters appearing in cartoon. At this point, Mr. Whitman suggested
that as long as we had the know-how, it might be a good idea
to form a company and do the job ourselves. He proposed a
plan whereby each would share in the profits according to his
contribution to the project. Mr. Wells became involved in the
conversation, apparently taking for granted that he was part

of the deal. He was promptly told by Mr. Whitman that he wouldn't have any interest in the company nor would either of his sons. The argument took on the complexion of a family squabble, ending with the two sons and Mr. Wells leaving, not in the best of humor. It was getting late, so the meeting broke up with a time set for further talks.

The two sons were at the next meeting, but they took no part. It was agreed that we incorporate as the Coliseum Film Producing Company, and I was flattered when I was elected the temporary president. As some money was necessary to have the incorporation papers drawn, each was willing to put up an equal amount, but Mr. Whitman generously offered to furnish the total himself. He also volunteered to do all the leg work required for he realized that all of us had jobs. Some money was also required to build the tracing stands to make the cartoon tracings that would be photographed as replacements for the fighters and, at the same time, make opaque tracings for the traveling printing matte. A friend of mine, Edward Gordon, had been bothering me for some time to find him an opportunity to invest in the movie business. It struck me that this might be the time, so I suggested that he put up the money for building the stands as well as pay for the rental of the cameras we would use to photograph the fight. This was agreeable to all, so my friend Gordon bought in. The responsibility was divided. I was to take care of photographing the fight, Hurd was to arrange for the tracings and to produce the finished combination of live action and cartoon negative ready to make the prints, Lyman was to act as a coordinator, and Gordon was to furnish any necessary cash. Of course, Whitman's part was as promoter of the project. The whole matter was to be kept in strict secrecy because of the governor's involvement.

We arranged to use a small laboratory in Cliffside, New Jersey, to make the tracings. I had made arrangements for the cameras and the cameramen to photograph the fight. About ten days before the fight, I told Whitman I would have to see where the fight ring was to be built in order to figure out the placing of the platforms for the cameras as soon as possible. A few days later he called for me at the studio, and I followed in my car to Madison Square Garden, where Tex Rickard had his offices. I waited for about twenty minutes. When Whitman returned, he told me that Tex was delighted with our interest in doing a good job and that in a few days it would be possible for me to visit the arena with the men who were going to construct the ring so that I could have them face the arena in any direction I wanted to get the best photography.

The following day I acquired about one hundred feet of positive film of the Dempsey-Brennon fight that had been photographed, I believe, in the old St. Nicholas fight club in uptown New York. I wanted to make a test. I stopped at Whitman's apartment on my way home to Fort Lee, New Jersey, to tell him that I had received the fight film and was going to make a test the next evening to see that no last minute bugs developed to stop us from getting the fight pictures out in a hurry.

The next night, when I was parked on the ferry boat about in the middle of the line of cars on my way home, a man I didn't recognize came alongside the car and asked if my name was Miller and I told him it was. Often people would pass among the cars on the boat and ask for a ride from the ferry to Fort Lee, where they could again meet the trolley car, thus saving them time if they were going further into New Jersey. I assumed that the stranger was one of those people and told him to get in because I was going as far as Fort Lee. His next words puzzled me, for he said, "I was told to tell you that if you have any fight picture film in your car to get rid of it. You're transporting it from one state to another." Almost before I realized what he said, he had disappeared. I couldn't be sure, but it seemed to me later that the voice was that of Mr. Wells, the man who had been at the first meeting in Whitman's apartment. As the ferry boat came close to the Jersey side, I slipped out of the car and from the rear of the boat I quietly dropped the can of film into the river. The boat docked and as I pulled off the ramp and out of the ferry house, two men beckoned to me to leave the line of cars. One fellow asked if I had any fight pictures in the car, while the other opened the back door and began searching. I was so amazed and dumbfounded that I didn't have the presence of mind to ask who they were. They finally told me to go ahead, which I did in a hurry.

As soon as I reached home, I telephoned Whitman at his apartment but got no answer. All evening I continued to call with the same results. The next morning I left for the studio early and stopped on Riverside Drive at Whitman's apartment. To my astonishment, the apartment was completely empty. The janitor told me that he had moved out last night and had left no forwarding address. At that point it dawned on me that I had been taken, but I couldn't understand why anyone would go to all that trouble for the few dollars involved.

About eleven o'clock that morning at the studio, I found out what was back of the deal. A fellow I knew, who worked in the Schulte cigar store on the corner of 44th or 45th Street and Broadway, came to the studio to ask me if he should add to the stock he had already bought from the Coliseum Film Producing Company. He understood that the company was going to photograph the Dempsey-Carpentier fight. He showed me a stock certificate that carried my name as president and he thought I could give him the dope first hand. The Whitmans had not been too successful in peddling the phony stock certificates and, we, the suckers, were taught a fairly inexpensive lesson, as it cost each of us about three thousand dollars before everything was settled. After I found out the whole deal was a bunco game, I surmised that the fellow who tipped me off to get rid of the film on the ferry boat doublecrossed a further shakedown by Whitman with the two fake government men who searched my car. The studio executive who was supposed to have sent Mr. Whitman to Lyman's department had never heard of him until I asked about him.

This was not the last I heard of these swindlers, for about five years later, when I was in California, my mother-in-law sent me a newspaper clipping from a Philadelphia paper. Mr. Whitman and his two sons had been convicted of a similar dishonest scheme, only this time they had become involved with someone much smarter than we were. Whitman senior was sentenced to five years in jail, while the sons got three years each.

Chapter 14

FILMING IN LONDON AND ROME

I N 1921 in the middle of July we sailed for London to make *Three Live Ghosts,* and we took Anna Q. Nilsson, Norman Kerry, and Eddie Goulding with us. Cyril Chadwick and the rest of the cast were English. *Three Live Ghosts* was a comedy about a man of noble birth who was suffering from amnesia as the result of having been shellshocked in the war. A character named Mrs. Gubbons, overly fond of liquor, and a couple of highbinders who were second-story men, looked after him. We worked at what is called the Islington studio which we found to be modern in all respects. I was kidded a great deal about my accent, but I enjoyed the friendly and helpful people at the studio. Alfred Hitchcock was the art director and needs no bouquets from me.

On one occasion I went along with him to a rather shabby residence where he spent some time bargaining with the woman of the house for all her old furniture to be replaced entirely by new. He used her old furniture to dress the set he had designed at the studio. Among the furnishings Hitchcock thus acquired was one article I never will forget. It was an old-fashioned wind-up phonograph and a few records, one of which was a vocal by a girl about "the monkey chews tobacco and spit some in my eye." The crew was enchanted with it and played it so often that all of us knew the lyrics by heart.

We made a number of candid shots in familiar spots in London with Chadwick dressed in morning clothes pushing a baby

Cyril Chadwick in *Three Live Ghosts* must have felt rather foolish, but few Londoners paid any attention, even though he was leading a reluctant lamb.

perambulator and crossing the streets in busy traffic. To do these, we used a lorry covered with a tarpaulin parked at the curb with the camera shooting through a peephole at the precise moment Chadwick was sent from his hiding place. This background material convinced audiences that the picture really had been made in London. Very few motion pictures were made there in 1921.

While we were still in London, Maurice Elvey directed a picture called *The Clock*, a mysterious, well-produced whodunit. My second cameraman, McDonald, was able to arrange a special screening so that I could see it before we left for Rome.

After we finished *Three Live Ghosts*, we had a long wait for Ouida Bergere to finish her next script, an adaptation from the play *The Man From Home*, which we planned to make in Rome. We started the picture there the latter part of October, 1921, with Anna Q. Nilsson and Norman Kerry again in the cast. The leading man, James Kirkwood, arrived from New York. For background, we tried to use as much of beautiful Rome as we could. One afternoon while we were working on a rather wide thoroughfare, we heard the sound of an approaching band. It wasn't long before the parade headed in our direction. We waited for quite a while but there seemed to be no end to it. The men in the parade wore hats resembling Turkish fezzes, with a white skull and crossbones on the front. Their black shirts also bore a similar emblem. They had blue-grey riding breeches that flared out at the pockets, black, shiny shoes, and almost knee-high, highly polished black puttees. The sight was impressive and hard to forget.

As the parade continued, our Italian property man kept repeating, "Il Duce, Il Duce," almost in a state of hypnosis. The line of black-shirted marchers occasionally stopped and, on command, gave a slightly upward straight-arm salute, as they loudly roared "Il Duce." That night in our hotel lobby there was much talk about what had taken place that day. The parade was Mussolini's entrance into Rome. The king had sent for him but Mussolini had refused to appear so the king instead had gone to see him. That night trucks loaded with these black-shirted men roamed the streets singing the Mussolini song "Giovanezza." We were warned that if a truck loaded with the black-shirted men went by to be sure to give the Fascist salute as the natives did or rocks might be sent our way from the trucks. Someone who probably had not heard this was standing in front of the Grand Hotel when two large plate glass windows were shattered by rocks from one of the passing trucks. The celebrating continued for the next three days. The attendant uncertainty of this situation caused us to rearrange our schedule so that we could leave Rome as fast as possible.

Only a week or so after we returned to New York (April, 1922), we were on our way to work at the Famous Players-Lasky studio in California. The studio was on the corner of Vine Street and Sunset Boulevard in Hollywood. Our first picture there was *To Have And To Hold*, with Betty Compson and Bert Lytell. Then we made Pola Negri's first two American pictures, *Bella Donna,* and *The Cheat,* a remake of the picture in which Sessue Hayakawa had told me he made his mark. Stories of Pola Negri's temperament had preceded her arrival, none of which were true, and, besides, Fitzmaurice had the kind of ability to which all temperaments responded.

C. B. DeMille was top man at the studio and I was flattered when one day in 1923 he sent for me. He told me that his next picture would be *The Ten Commandments* and wanted to know if I would be interested in photographing it. After a few more meetings with Mr. DeMille that Fitzmaurice knew nothing about, I signed a one-year contract with options. Everything was settled when I left the office, but I came face to face with Fitzmaurice who had sensed what had taken place and confronted me with his suspicions. Then Fitzmaurice said he had just signed a contract to make pictures for Sam Goldwyn, the first to be made in Rome, and had counted on my going with him. I was ashamed of having concluded the whole deal with Mr. DeMille without having first discussed it with Fitz. My remorse was so strong that I returned to Mr. DeMille's office and told him how I felt. He opened the drawer of his desk, took out the six signed copies of the contract, gently tore them into little pieces, and dropped them into the wastepaper basket. Then he looked me straight in the eye and said, "I can appreciate your feelings." Then he added in a matter-of-fact way, "Well, perhaps some other time."

Within a week I had purchased a Mitchell camera to use in Rome for the Sam Goldwyn company. The Mitchell was new on the market and had one feature that was an innovation. Like the Bell & Howell, the Mitchell had the same convenient turret with openings for the placement of a selection of four lenses, but with the Bell & Howell after viewing through the lens to compose a picture, before shooting, the turret had to be revolved one half turn to place the lens in front of the photographing aperture. To compensate for the lens adjustment, the camera had to slide the same distance in the dovetailed slot of the tilt, which was part of the tripod head. This entailed pushing out the matte box on the two round rods extending from the tripod head. After the camera had been positioned, the matte box had to be slid back. A last, quick look through the lens was out of the question because of the time involved. The cameraman had to depend on what he saw in the finder, taking into consideration the problem of parallax, to answer all last-minute questions as to whether this was in or out of the picture. With the Mitchell camera, the turret remained in the same position after turning it and selecting the desired lens. The housing that encased the pull-down pins and the photographing aperture, as well as the ground glass and viewing optics, also carried the film magazines on top. Simply by releasing the locking pin by pressing the thumb in the center of a bar that the first two fingers conveniently grasped, the camera housing slid across behind the turret to the photographing position with a twist of the wrist. The photographing aperture was behind the lens. The whole maneuver took about one second. This allowed the cameraman that precious last second look directly through the lens, eliminating the hazard of parallax. Last-minute questions, such as, "Will this be in the picture when you pan over here?" could be answered promptly and with positive assurance. There is no doubt that the Mitchell camera was then and is now a wonderful piece of precision equipment; however, in my opinion, the rack-over feature, as it was called when the camera was first placed on the market, was a big factor in its success. In a short time, it replaced the Bell & Howell camera with its ingenious shuttle movement and rugged construction. It must be remembered that the individual cameraman made the choice of camera in those days, and a great number bought and maintained their own.

In her screen adaptation of *The Eternal City*, Ouida Bergere had changed the story to interject Mussolini and the Fascist movement. Mussolini was so impressed with the idea that his office was open to us at any time. We were assigned several of his black-shirt men to hold the crowds back, especially when we worked in small mountain towns. They did anything we asked of them. One Sunday we shot in five different locations in Rome, walking two thousand extras from one location to another and ending at the Coliseum. Not long after that when I was in Mussolini's office, I asked him if I could take a picture of him. He agreed and sat behind his desk for the portrait without asking any questions. Mussolini spoke English very slowly and in a soft voice. Considering the man he was in 1924 and what he had done in the short time he had been in power since our first visit to Rome to convert from steam to electric railroads, remove the great number of beggars from the streets, the new cleanliness of Rome, and the drastic change in the attitude of its citizens, it is difficult to understand how he could have turned into such a despicable individual.

The choice of locations captured the essence of Rome and made *The Eternal City* a most memorable picture. Less than a week's shooting remained to be done when one evening Mr. Brunner, the company's business manager, came to my hotel room to tell me that Fitzmaurice was leaving for New York the next day. He told me that I was to stay on a week or more to shoot some added scenes for a riot sequence we had taken in the ancient ruins of a Roman bath. Arturo Caluci, who had been working with us on the picture helping with mob scenes, was to direct these scenes. The story sounded peculiar to me for I knew that under normal circumstances Fitz would not leave without first giving me some idea of what we were to shoot. The business manager asked me not to say anything to anyone about Fitzmaurice leaving, which added to my suspicions. I asked Mr. Brunner if he knew that there were about two thousand feet of developed negative still at the laboratory that I hadn't shipped. As soon as he heard this, Brunner became concerned and gave me the real story. It seems that Mussolini had looked at the picture we had made on our last visit to Rome called *The Man From Home*. It appeared to him that the picture ridiculed Italian nobility, and he was furious and wanted to see Fitzmaurice. I am not sure, but I have always thought that Fitzmaurice had already left Italy when Mr. Brunner was talking to me. At any rate, Brunner suggested I go to the lab, pick up the three cans of negative, put them in our wardrobe trunk, take my wife and luggage and go down to Venice for a few weeks, and from there go home alone.

We had a total of four trunks, plus the Mitchell camera in its case, which accompanied us in our compartment in the train and in the stateroom of the *Aquitania*. The one trunk that seemed most attractive to customs men and was examined at each border was the one filled with wardrobe used in the picture. Only once did they open the trunk that contained the negative film, which was on the bottom in one of the drawers and was covered with wearing apparel. Usually one, or at the most two, of the trunks was opened. When nothing dutiable was found, an "X" was made on all four trunks. I'm sure we could have come through the customs in New York, too, but the Goldwyn company had a broker there to take care of things, with the result that everything went to the customs house for examination, once they declared the negative film. In this instance, Mr. Brunner saved the day, for if the black-shirt boys had gotten their hands on the film that would have been the end of it. We finished up by photographing the interiors of the picture in the 48th Street studio in New York.

Goldwyn's next production, *Cytherea*, starred Lewis Stone, Alma Rubens, and Irene Rich. Constance Bennett had a small part. Goldwyn was using the vacant Biograph studio in New York, since by this time Fort Lee had seen about the last of motion picture studio production and the migration to California was beginning to take its toll of the few studios in New York. The Biograph studio, taken over by Klaw and Erlanger, had begun to deteriorate and was in a sorry condition. Neither the lighting equipment nor anything else had been maintained, and to do a fair day's work was impossible. Try as we might, conditions didn't improve, so in November, 1923, Goldwyn stopped production there and moved bag and baggage to the West Coast. He rented studio space at the Brunton lot in Hollywood, the same studio where I had shot the two pictures with Sessue Hayakawa. This was my third trip to California and this time I knew it would become my permanent home.

Mr. Goldwyn had made an arrangement with the Technicolor Corporation to shoot two sequences of *Cytherea* in color, he to be sole judge as to whether the color was satisfactory and, if so, he would use the color sequences in the picture.

Technicolor sent Mr. J. A. Ball, an official of the company as well as technical expert on the process, as their representative. There were no exposure meters, so in order to arrive at the density of negative required, we made hand tests in a test box of the type used by most cameramen, especially when away from the studio on location. For the first time, Technicolor was to be photographed with artificial light. We were restricted to arc light only and, by the time the light level had been built up to a point satisfactory to Mr. Ball, we had added several sun arcs and, if the actors had not started grumbling about the excessive heat, we might have used even more. Two days were required to struggle through the two sequences, but the result was well worth the effort, for the color sequences added greatly to the picture. It seems to me that in the following year Irwin Willat directed and Ray Rennahan photographed *Wanderer of the Wasteland,* a Paramount full-length feature, entirely in Technicolor.

By the end of 1924 Goldwyn had produced and Fitzmaurice directed, *Tarnish, A Thief in Paradise,* and *His Supreme Moment,* all starring Goldwyn's new acquisition, Ronald Colman, and again proving Goldwyn's ability to choose star material. In the last-named picture Blanche Sweet was the leading lady. I had admired her for a long time, but this was the first occasion on which I had the pleasure of photographing her. Like everyone else, I had my favorites, and Miss Sweet was certainly one of them.

Fitzmaurice had gone off to New York and while he was away, our little agreement expired. Abe Lehr, Goldwyn's manager, came to me and wanted to talk contract. I didn't want to go through another embarrassing experience such as I underwent when I signed with C. B. DeMille so I wired Fitzmaurice but received no answer. My disappointment must have been quite evident when by chance I encountered Anna Q. Nilsson on the lot. She remarked that I looked as if the world were about to come to an end and asked what the trouble was. I told her, and she asked if I were still interested in working with Mr. DeMille. For some reason, I always had felt that to work with DeMille meant that one had reached the top of his profession and at this moment the opportunity sounded most inviting. Miss Nilsson sensed my interest and told me that Mr.

DeMille was leaving Paramount to start his own company. He intended to take over the old Ince studio in Culver City. The more she talked, the more the idea appealed to me and I asked her how to go about it. She said, "You wait here and I'll find out when he can see you." After talking to Mr. DeMille on the phone, she told me that he would be glad to see me in his office in Culver City at five o'clock that afternoon. Mr. DeMille's office was very impressive and was decorated with many trophies from his hunting trips, including a huge black bear rug on the floor in front of his desk. We chatted for about half an hour, with DeMille doing most of the talking. He made one statement that I was to be reminded of some time later. "This time, Arthur, there won't be any getting out of the contract," DeMille said jokingly, as I left his office. Two days later I signed for three years.

The contract was not due to go into effect for about seven weeks, so my wife and I made an automobile trip across the country to New York, taking the script of *The Volga Boatman*, the first picture Mr. DeMille planned to make, along with me. When we returned, we started shooting exteriors along the Sacramento River, which was intended to represent the Volga, while the company lived in one of the small towns nearby. The cast included Bill Boyd, Elinor Fair (she and Bill Boyd were secretly married while the picture was being made), Victor Varconi, Jetta Goudal, Theodore Kosloff, and others.

Some of the cameramen were using panchromatic film on exteriors, particularly when shooting night shots in the daytime. I, too, had made several tests and had decided to use this film on the night scenes that were to be shot in the daytime. This had the advantage of allowing one to shoot a blue sky with a proper filter and end up with a dark sky, thereby simulating night. The orthochromatic film we had used for years had the disadvantage of reproducing a blue sky as white. To photograph the close-ups with panchromatic required alterations in makeup, so whenever the sky area of the picture could be eliminated or blocked out with brush or trees, it was advisable to use the old orthochromatic film and thus avoid the necessity for changing makeup. The best results, of course, came from using panchromatic film for everything, but the time element was also of importance.

The use of panchromatic film, the problems it presented in alteration of makeup, the time involved, and the whole procedure was covered thoroughly with Mr. DeMille before we left the Culver City studio. However, when we started shooting on location, either altering the makeup or reloading the camera with ortho film seemed to annoy him considerably. Before we finished the location work, I knew I had made a serious mistake. Up to this time it always had been my responsibility to photograph the picture, of course after consulting the director, but never before had I encountered a group of persons who loudly expressed their opinions on the result. Oddly enough, their opinions turned out to be identical with those of Mr. DeMille, once he had decided what course to follow.

The one incident that completely disenchanted me occurred when the first positive prints of the film we had shot arrived and a small theater in town was chosen to show them after the regular evening performance. The program that night at the theater was *The Merry Widow*, which had been photographed in low-key lighting. I had gone to see the film a few nights earlier and noticed then that the light in the projector was weak and that, combined with the low-key lighting of *The Merry Widow,* meant that hardly an image was visible on the screen. The night we ran our film, it appeared flat, dull, and without sparkle, all of which was due to the lack of light in the projector. The laboratory had sent along the light tests together with the film, a usual practice even when working at the studio. From these, as well as the film, anyone with the slightest knowledge of film production could see that the fault lay in the projection.

In spite of this, everyone expressed such concern and doubt about what we had seen that the business manager had to route out of bed the manager of one of the better theaters in Sacramento, some eighty miles from where we were, so that we could run the film there at about three o'clock in the morning. With proper projection, it was obvious to all that nothing was wrong with the film. What dumbfounded me was that the anxiety of the group disappeared and all expressed great relief, but not until Mr. DeMille had decided that the film was all right.

After we returned to the studio and as the film progressed, it became increasingly clear that any effort I made would be nullified by the strained relationship. Everybody had more to say about photographing the picture than the person whose job it was. About ten days before the picture was finished, I asked Mr. DeMille to cancel our contract. He then repeated the words, "I told you there would be no getting out of this contract." I insisted on being replaced, and in a few days another cameraman took over, my punishment being that the photographic credit for *The Volga Boatman* was split with the man who had replaced me. For the remainder of the three-year contract, most of the pictures I photographed starred Leatrice Joy, which pleased us both. A few of the films starred Bill Boyd, Rod LaRocque, or Joe Schildkraut. I am sure Mr. DeMille had the last word on all those pictures, but he personally directed none of them.

I was farmed out to M.G.M., once to make *The Bellamy Trial,* with Leatrice Joy, while the other picture, *The High Road,* starred both Ruth Chatterton and Basil Rathbone. These two pictures were released by M.G.M.

Many changes came to the moving picture industry during the three years the DeMille studio was in existence. Panchromatic negative had been manufactured by the Eastman Kodak Company and used on special occasions as early as 1919. In 1922 Ned Van Buren photographed *The Headless Horseman,* starring Will Rogers, using a special coated batch of panchromatic negative emulsion, number 1227. It wasn't until 1925, however, that cameramen in general began experimenting with the testing panchromatic negative. At the same time, experiments began with incandescent lights. Since panchromatic negative was sensitive to all colors, it provided an opportunity to use a wide range of filters that opened the door to new adventures in motion picture photography.

Thomas Edison had always worked toward pictures to match his talking and musical records. Strangely enough, the success of the combination happened the other way around when, in

Director Monta Bell standing on bench, Leatrice Joy in witness box, assistant cameraman taping footage for focus, and Arthur Miller at Mitchell camera. Betty Bronson in foreground. Scene from M. G. M.'s *The Bellamy Trial*.

1927, Warner Brothers made phonograph records to match their pictures. They produced several reels of talking pictures that I remember seeing at the Egyptian Theater in Hollywood. One was a singing trio appearing with Paul Whiteman's band at the Ambassador Hotel; another was Georgie Jessel doing his famous telephone conversation with his mother. These were amusing novelty reels but aroused no special interest. A feature followed that was filled with sound effects. One I particularly recall registered the shrill scream of Louise Fazenda. Then came the talking picture that stirred Hollywood, *The Jazz Singer*, with Al Jolson. When the scene where he played the piano was finished, he turned to his mother and said, "How do you like that, mama?" This was really the beginning of talking pictures. The novelty aspect had gone. Here was the sound of the voice replacing written conversational titles. After the preview, the main topic in Hollywood was talking pictures. The smart producers had a feeling "talkies," as they were called, were here to stay. There were a few diehards who insisted that it was a fad and would run its course, but the scramble was on. Several producers were looking for equipment to get on the bandwagon.

The DeMille studio, not to be left behind, ordered their sound equipment from the R.C.A. laboratories, and with it came four men. I was in Annapolis, Maryland, at the Naval Academy, making a picture with John Mack Brown as its star. We were staying at Carvel Hall when a wire came for me from the studio. To me it is a classic for it read "Crank 24. We are going to use sound in this picture." This was a pretty short explanation of the momentous change that was taking place. That evening at the hotel I practiced cranking my camera at twenty four frames per second. Sixteen was normal, so this made three turns per second instead of two. We photographed the cadets marching on the parade grounds, cranking twenty four in accordance with the instructions. For other scenes in the picture, I still cranked sixteen. After the editor ran some of the parade scenes at the studio, I received a wire from him asking if something had gone wrong with my camera as the parading cadets seemed to be marching a bit slow. To play it safe, we made some more scenes of the parading cadets, cranking the camera at the normal speed of sixteen.

When we returned to the studio, the place was in a turmoil. The men who had come with the sound equipment were in full charge, and their decisions overrode all other activities, as sound was the main objective and nothing else mattered. Many changes had to be made before the sound equipment could be utilized. All the walls of the stage had to be covered with felt to deaden the echoes. We had a head start on the use of incandescent light for photographing when we started partial use of panchromatic film some two years earlier, but there were still a good number of arc lights in use, especially the overhead spotlights, the noise of which could not be tolerated when recording dialogue. Sheets of asbestos were wrapped around them to deaden the popping sound when the tin housing became hot. The camera noise also had to be silenced. This was accomplished by building a triangular-shaped soundproof booth to accommodate the spread of the tripod legs, and a piece

of 8″x10″ plate glass was provided for the camera to photograph through. The motor was connected to the camera by a
flexible shaft. The idea was that as the motor started at top
speed, the flexible shaft would alleviate the sudden jerk. The
cameraman had to arrange the camera for the shot, get out of
the booth, and close the door. When all was ready, he flipped
the switch outside the booth and started the camera rolling.
When the scene was over and the camera opened, it was often
found that the belt on the take-up side of the film magazine
did not take up the film fast enough to accommodate the sudden jerk at the beginning, and allowed the film to jam and pile
up like the bellows of an accordion inside the camera. This
was called a "buckle," and the film piled up until the roller
guides at the top and bottom of the sprockets were so badly
sprung that the camera had to be sent to the shop to have the
film removed and be repaired. Finally, a buckle switch was
devised that cut the electricity when the film started to buckle.
The wear and tear put a premium on Mitchell cameras and
practically every cameraman who owned one sold it to some
studio.

Since Warner Brothers' sound was recorded on a phonograph
disc, the sound track couldn't be cut. Eight or ten cameras
were used to photograph an entire scene; long shot, medium,
and close-ups. Each camera operator was instructed as to what
part of the action he was to photograph, so the editors were
well supplied with angles for editing the scene. One thousand-
foot film magazines had become a necessity, for many of the
scenes ran between eight hundred and one thousand feet. All
cameras were interlocked with the motor running the sound-
cutting head, and everything was synchronized to start rolling
together. Once started, all cameras ran without interruption
through the entire scene. To cut out one, that perhaps might
be photographing only a shot that was going to be used for as
little as twenty feet, could cause a surge of power and spoil
the entire take. At the beginning of talkies at the DeMille
studio, although we recorded sound on film, we were instructed
to follow the same procedure—all cameras were to run continually throughout the entire scene.

The DeMille studio had built new booths with a bench about waist high where three cameras could be mounted. A large piece of plate glass, extending from the bench up, formed the front of the booth. The glass slanted in toward the bottom and a shelf projected about fourteen inches outside the booth at bench height. The shelf was covered with black velvet from which the glass took its reflection. From the inside, it was not possible to tell the glass was there. Up to this time, sound men had always insisted that the microphone, even when actors were moving and talking, be placed just above their heads. And of course, the directors couldn't have the actors always standing still for dialogue. To solve the problem, the sound men devised the following procedure. The microphone was tied to the end of a piece of cord that ran on a pulley through a pulley block which was fastened to the end of a piece of 2' x 4' and was extended from the top of the set as close to the center of the general action as possible. A man on the catwalk that supported the overhead lights could take in or let out the cord, thereby lowering or raising the microphone to whatever height was required at any time. Four more pieces of cord were fastened to the microphone, each to be guided by a man placed at each corner of the set on the catwalk. As an actor moved in any direction, the man to whom he moved would take in his cord.

This naturally would move the microphone in an upward curve so that the man controlling the up and down movement would let out on his cord to compensate and keep the microphone at the same height. If this sounds like a lot of foolish nonsense, it was. To watch these five men trying to coordinate the movement of the microphone while following the actors seemed senseless. We made take after take and accomplished very little in a day. When we viewed the rushes, it was not unusual to see the microphone dip into a scene, and the one who did the most screaming was the director, who was in the least position to help or prevent it. The motion picture business hadn't grown out of the days when everything was improvised to take care of each situation as it came along. The workmen on the set did the improvising, and finally the head of the department would come up with some kind of a permanent gadget to take care of the problem from then on. So it was when sound came in.

The same workmen built the microphone boom so that one man could control the microphone from position to position. They built the booths and even the blimps that housed one camera and could be moved around on a tripod. The most urgent and useful piece of equipment was the microphone boom, for it wasn't long before the cameraman and the boom man were cooperating with each other and planning the shots to be made. The grips began building flags and cutters to take care of the shadows of the microphone on the walls. The cameraman started taking into consideration the placement of the microphone boom stand when he lighted the shot and contemplated the shadows that would have to be eliminated from the boom arm and microphone as it moved around the set to record dialogue. The operator of the camera worked out with the boom operator how high the microphone would have to go to be out of the picture at different positions in the set. The editors had devised ways of cutting the film sound track, and smaller blimps were built to silence the camera that could be moved around from place to place. Electrical supply houses built all kinds of incandescent lighting equipment which made little or no noise, and it wasn't long before the moving picture industry had eliminated all of the real problems of making talking pictures and were back to what they considered normal.

Chapter 15

WITH CECIL B. DeMILLE
AND JOHN FORD

THE PERIOD FROM 1925 to 1929 is considered by most cinematographers to be the murderous years. I don't believe there ever was or ever will be a time when the employer in the motion picture business showed less consideration for those he employed than in this period. It really began about the middle of 1924. A company, under some pretense or another of emergency, would be called back after dinner. The "emergency" might be to have an actor finish his part or to kill a set. No matter what the excuse, the company worked until eleven o'clock at night. This happened on the Brunton lot where I was working at the time. Nothing was ever said about extra compensation for the extra hours worked. The so-called emergencies grew more frequent throughout the industry until some companies were including Wednesday nights until eleven in the shooting schedule of their pictures. Then Saturday nights were added and that usually meant working until daybreak after a full day. By 1927, the industry-wide practice for the remaining days in the week was to have a paper cup of hot chocolate or coffee and a ham and egg sandwich brought in for the crew, which they ate during a twenty-minute "rest period." One studio was really big-hearted and handed out dinner checks acceptable in a few of the local restaurants in the amount of one dollar. After dinner, we returned to the studio and worked until nine or ten o'clock, according to the number of scenes we shot. Some relatives of the management, who had key production jobs, would call from home during the evening to find out how much the company had accomplished and, if it suited them, would OK quitting time.

Talk of forming a union began to be discussed among cameramen, some of whom objected violently. The dissenters felt it to be below the dignity of a creative group such as ours. Finally the abuses became so flagrant and the hours so unbearable that something just had to be done. Despite the threats and intimidation by some of the underlings of the different studios, the cameramen formed a union affiliated with the A. F. of L. It took the wholehearted assistance and cooperation of the camera and other craft unions, especially those operating out of New York City who covered the places we went for distant locations, to convince the producers that it would be to their advantage to sit down and talk things over.

The bargaining sessions that followed finally concluded in a contract agreement between us. The agreement stipulated a minimum wage but, more important, also the working hours and conditions. The cameramen tried for a maximum sixty-hour work week to start but had to compromise for what was more valuable, a first working agreement. The producers held out for a paragraph that included the words "in case of an emergency," which meant that they could call anything they chose an emergency, especially money. As expected, quite a few producers attempted to make their entire picture under this emergency clause. A few years later, the cameramen succeeded in having a clause put in the contract to the effect that a triple-time penalty would be imposed for any work required over sixteen continuous hours. Gradually contracts have been negotiated over the years to a point where I believe there is a sincere cooperative spirit between the film producers and the photographic branch of the industry. Of course, some of the adamant old guard producers have disappeared from the scene, making the change possible. This tale of woe is related only because then and now some people wonder why a group of creative men who are continually competing with each other in a truly artistic sense found it necessary to form a union. The truth is that it was forced on them by circumstances.

The last picture I photographed for the DeMille company was *His First Command,* starring Bill Boyd. The locale of the story was Fort Riley, Kansas, so we went there to make the picture. Our company lived at a small hotel in Manhattan, Kansas, about six or seven miles from the fort. We were in the heart of the beautiful farming and dairy country of Kansas, and on our way to the fort each morning, we passed farm after farm where the milk cans were stacked at the gates waiting to be picked up and delivered to a central place where the milk was then bottled and distributed to the market. I drank more than my share of this wonderful, rich, fresh, unpasteurized milk, and in about two weeks I felt rather sluggish and not quite myself. After we returned to the studio and had finished the picture, my health continued to fail and finally I went to the hospital. It is now known that some persons who drink unpasteurized milk from a cow infected with Bang's disease develop undulant fever. This is what happened to me and, unfortunately, very little was known about undulant fever at the time.

After several months I felt well enough to work, and the first picture to come my way was *See America Thirst* with Harry Langdon and Slim Summerville at the Universal studio. This was followed by one with Helen Twelvetrees directed by Tay Garnett and, of all the studios, it was produced at the DeMille lot, now called the Pathé studio. At this time it was, in some way, tied up with R.K.O., and Joseph P. Kennedy, father of the late president, was the head man. Erich Von Stroheim was working at the studio making a picture with Gloria Swanson called *Queen Kelly;* however, something happened and production was stopped before the picture was completed. I can't recall any other company working there at the time.

After this came *Panama Flo,* again starring Helen Twelvetrees with Charles Bickford in the male lead, and another at R.K.O. with the same actress, which William Seiter directed. My next assignment was also with Seiter at the Warner Brothers studio where I photographed a picture starring the young

and beautiful Loretta Young. Warner Brothers was still recording sound on a phonograph disc, which meant shooting each
individual scene with about ten cameras, all running at the
same time from different angles. Under these circumstances,
quality photography was impossible to achieve. I kept hopping
from one studio to another without much rest in between. A
free-lancer was either on or off the merry-go-round and once
he got off, there were often long stretches before getting on
again. The only thing that kept a free-lance cinematographer
working was knowing a few stars or directors.

The next picture took me to the Universal studio to photograph *Okay America*. This time Tay Garnett was the director
for Lew Ayres who played a fast-talking newspaper reporter
and radio broadcaster, a la Walter Winchell. In this picture,
his first, Edward Arnold took the part of a Chicago gangster.
He did such an excellent job in the role that he became a star
and went on to make pictures like *Diamond Jim,* and so on. I
had just finished the picture when I received a telephone call
from someone at the Fox company asking me to meet Raoul
Walsh on a certain street in Pasadena, California, where he
was shooting a location. I had seen a great many pictures Walsh
had directed but had never met him. When I arrived I talked
a few minutes to the cameraman who was shooting the picture
and he told me that this was the last day of shooting. I was
then introduced to Mr. Walsh who, without preamble, asked
me if I were the Miller who had worked with George Fitzmaurice. I told him I was. Evidently Walsh had no time to
spare in idle conversation and wanted to get back to work, so
with a quick response to my answer, he said, "Report to the
studio some time in the morning and I'll get you fixed up to
shoot my next picture. It was nice seeing you," and he left
to go back to work. The next morning I waited in the Fox
studio in the camera department, but as time wore on and Mr.
Walsh didn't put in an appearance, the head of the department
started talking about salary, with the understanding that I was
to be paid beginning that morning. I saw nothing of Walsh
for the entire week. Finally his assistant came to the camera
department with a script and said Walsh wanted me to read

it and that we would start shooting in about two weeks. In the interim I was to make myself acquainted with the studio. The working title of the script was *Pier Thirteen,* but this later was changed to *Me and My Gal,* with Spencer Tracy and Joan Bennett as the stars. Raoul Walsh's years of experience made working with him a pleasurable association. The mysterious manner he used to select me as photographer for his picture was solved when one day he told me about it. It seems that when he was about to make the picture *Rain,* released as *Sadie Thompson* late in 1928 with Gloria Swanson, he was looking for a cameraman. His production designer, Billy Menzies, had suggested me. I was not available at the time but Walsh said he had never forgotten what Billy had told him about me and my work as a cameraman.

Me and My Gal was the first picture I photographed at the Fox studio, and I remained there for the next eighteen years. Certain pictures and persons during those eighteen years have left distinct impressions. One of these was *The Pigskin Parade,* a comedy football story with a cast that included Judy Garland in perhaps her first picture; Betty Grable, with a small part; Stu Erwin, Jack Haley, Patsy Kelly, Tony Martin, and the Yacht Club Boys, one of whom is a successful TV director today. One of the football players in the film was an All-American from the University of Southern California, Aaron Rosenberg, now a film producer with such pictures as *Mutiny on the Bounty* to his credit. David Butler directed the picture. Butler also directed the first Shirley Temple picture *Bright Eyes* that I photographed. The producer was Sol Wurtzel. *Bright Eyes* and all the rest of the Shirley Temples that followed, I enjoyed immensely. I don't believe there will ever be another child actress with her exceptional talent; she was an adorable little pixie. Mrs. Temple deserves much credit for keeping Shirley a well-mannered child who respected her elders in spite of the fuss made over her. This is more than I can say about some with whom I worked.

Shirley had a most remarkable capacity to study and remember, not only her own, but also the lines of the actor or actress with whom she would be playing scenes. On those occasions

Shirley Temple
and
Arthur Miller.

when an actor blew his lines, Shirley would innocently say, "You're supposed to say . . ." but that's as far as she got before Mother, on the sidelines, would call "Shirley," and that stopped any further prompting. Mrs. Temple realized that some actors resented the help that Shirley volunteered.

Nearly every picture had a scene where Shirley was distressed for some reason or another, causing tears to well in her eyes and for her to sob. For these scenes, Mrs. Temple took Shirley to one side and got her in the mood by playing the same game which had been used many times before and which Shirley thoroughly understood. Shirley would think how terrible it would be if her little Pekingese, Ming Toy, were hurt. I often wondered what adult actresses thought of to get themselves in a crying mood. Shirley's method was no secret. The whole crew knew it and would go on with their work as quietly as possible. At this moment Shirley was treated as an adult. When she felt that she was ready to cry and sob, she would deliberately walk to her position where the scene had been re-hearsed, and usually two cameras, one medium and the close-up, would roll and the scene would be shot. In a few minutes of standing on the sidelines by herself after the scene was finished, Shirley reverted to the cheerful, happy child she normally was.

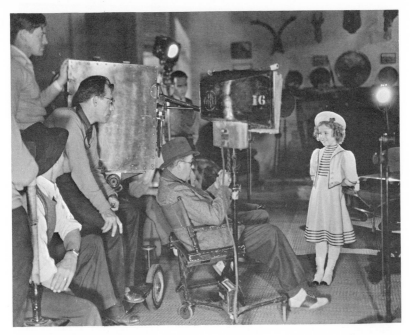

Shirley Temple was extremely fond of John Ford which is obvious in this picture as she listens to him. Miller profiled against the blimp that houses a Mitchell camera.

When I heard that John Ford was to direct Shirley in *Wee Willie Winkie,* I wondered if I would get the assignment, even though I had photographed several of Shirley's previous pictures. In 1935 when I saw *The Informer,* which Ford directed, I formed an opinion that he used photography as he did dialogue, to tell a story. I saw every picture he made after that and was convinced I was right. I had also become aware that Mr. Ford was rather particular when it came to his choice of a cameraman; therefore, it was gratifying when the production office told me Ford had asked for me for *Wee Willie Winkie.*

There were some concessions to be made when photographing Shirley, particularly as to the amount of light she could stand and where it was obligatory to place the lamps to supply that light. It was necessary to play the key or main light high out of her line of vision — otherwise it could be seen that she was straining to keep her eyes open. At times this meant some sacrifice in lighting for the person playing the scene with her. For a filler light, I used a small lamp that was built for use in still picture portrait studios. It had a 250 watt bulb with the front painted black, so that the only light from it was reflected from a white surface which formed the back of the lamp housing. On the back of the small lamp I used was a rheostat with a knob which I turned to control the intensity of the light. We played a little game in which Shirley would tell me how bright the light could be before it made her squint. She had fun teasing before she made up her mind.

This type of light, on a much larger scale, is widely used today in filming TV shows that are photographed using the multiple-camera system. Ordinarily three cameras are used, all rolling at the same time. The main camera is in the center, with a camera on either side picking out medium shots and close-ups, while the center camera covers long and semi-long shots. Of course, all cameras move in and out according to a well-rehearsed plan. Many of these shows are photographed before an audience. Indirect lighting, as it is now called, is useful on these shows, as the cameras photograph from all angles, and this type of lamp gives off a reflected soft general light that reduces unwanted shadows to a minimum.

When we shot close-ups on exteriors, we blocked out the sky and everything in back of the camera with a large piece of black cloth to make it easier for Shirley to keep her eyes open, and used booster light positioned as if in the studio. It took a lot of fussing, but in the long run it was the quickest way to do the job. Several persons who claimed to be in the know told me that John Ford wouldn't stand for all this fussing, implying that I had some problems to solve. Since I knew that none of these individuals had ever worked for Ford, I wondered how they could know so much about how he worked and decided to discount most of the volunteered suggestions.

I first met Mr. Ford on the test stage. We were to make a test of Victor McLaglen in his dress uniform of pith helmet, khaki jacket, and kilts. Shirley was a miniature replica standing beside him. After we made one shot as they stood, each making one full turn finishing facing the camera, Ford dismissed them.

That was the complete test. This was a great departure from the general routine I had experienced of making a test for any picture. Usually an important scene or two was selected from the script; the scene was played and rehearsed until the action and dialogue were as nearly perfect as possible, and then it was photographed. Medium shots and close-ups were made for the editor to put together the scene. If it was an important picture, these tests would be discussed by many well-meaning individuals for days. There isn't much to discuss about a test of two people turning around. I used the new Fox silent camera, still in the building and checking-out stage, to make the test. I understand that Charlie Miller (no relation) was the inventor of the camera and was present to watch its operation. Mr. Ford showed a keen interest in the new silent camera and asked Charlie several questions about it.

Ford then told me to pick up a script at his office, remarking, "be sure to read it." The Fox camera had a turret of lenses, as did the Mitchell and the Bell & Howell, but instead of racking over the housing that encased the photographing aperture and the pull-down mechanism, as was true with the Mitchell, the Fox camera rocked at a cental point from the straight up photographing position to the left and down to the viewing position. This all-important feature could be performed as fast as with the Mitchell. The optics in the finder moved automatically to take care of the parallax as the focus was changed on the photographing lens. The camera was provided with a slating device to change the scene numbers in the same manner as the date is changed on a rubber stamp. When the number block, about 2¼″ x 1½″, was in its place, the assistant pressed a handle to bring the number up in front of the lens, and when the camera was started and was building up to speed, this film, formerly wasted, now recorded the number of the scene. True, the camera at this stage needed frequent attention and sometimes while working on interiors, it had to be sent to the shop for a few days to be repaired, but after the camera was perfected, Fox built ten more. I am under the impression that this was the only attempt to build a silent professional moving picture camera in the United States.

When sound came in and had advanced to the point that individual blimps were built to house the Mitchell camera to contain the noise, the cameraman lost that great advantage of a last quick look through the lens simply by racking the camera over. With the camera housed in a blimp we weren't any further advanced than when we were using the Bell & Howell with its awkward routine of changing from the viewing position to the photographing position, as we still had to open the door and go through the entire rigmarole. As a matter of fact, we were worse off with the camera in the large blimp and the finder attached outside, five or six inches from the photographing lens, as it caused a horrible parallax situation.

After we had been working on the picture a short while, I learned two things. One, never to expect praise or flattery from Ford and two, never try to flatter him. I witnessed one attempt by an actor and Ford showed his resentment in no subtle manner. Much has been written about this man and his work, generalizing or trying to compare him with this or that director. After working with him for some time, I realized what an impossible task it was to describe his work, because when John Ford made a picture, he could not be compared even to himself from one day to the next. He was one hundred percent unpredictable and had no special method or formula for proceeding. Only one thing is certain and that is that Ford made the pictures himself without any interference.

There is a story that hardly needs repeating, but for the amusement of those who haven't heard it, and to eliminate any doubt that it actually happened, it goes like this. One of the would-be executives from the production office appeared where we were working on the back lot. Such appearances were so unusual, unless they were summoned, that Ford's attention was attracted and he beckoned the executive to him. Ford was sitting in his chair with the script on his lap. As the executive approached, Ford asked what was on his mind. The man explained that they had just held a production meeting and had reached the conclusion that the picture was four days behind schedule. Without changing his expression, Ford looked at him for a few seconds, and then casually opened the script, tore out four pages, handed them to the astounded man, and said, "We're on schedule. Now beat it."

My own opinion of John Ford's method of making a picture is that the script he works from is no more than an idea. He concentrates on making a completed picture, and to do so, he is continually prepared to deviate from the script whenever an idea strikes him. For this reason, the entire cast was required to be present each day, whether or not they worked, so that he could change or improve or add someone to a sequence without having to wait for the actor or to abandon the idea.

When we shot interiors, the only procedure that might be called routine was the morning session at a large coffee table. He and the cast would discuss anything from football to aviation. Along the line, Ford would gently interject something concerning one or two of the characters in the picture, without addressing his remarks directly to those who were playing the parts, but he made his point and would start the actors thinking. There were never any long rehearsals of a scene, especially of the dialogue, nor did I ever see him act a piece of business for an actor, or tell him when to look at someone, or read a line. There were no marks on the floor for the actors to position themselves; he simply gave them a general idea of where to be. I heard Ford tell a writer that if he gave detailed instructions to the actors that he, the writer, tried to write into script, all he would get would be a well-rehearsed line of chatter. I am sure that this is the reason he never had drilled rehearsals and was displeased when he had to make a second take of a scene, which he seldom did.

When something accidentally happens in a scene that hasn't been rehearsed, most directors stop the scene and begin again. In such an event, Ford always let the scene play to its conclusion and often the mishap resulted in a bit of realism. Sometimes he made use of the accident to develop a piece of humor. On a bright, sunshiny day when we were shooting a scene on the parade ground, Shirley had to look up at McLaglen and, as she did, the sun glared in her eyes. Instinctively, she shaded her eyes with her hand and continued playing the scene. Mrs. Temple inquired if that was all right. Ford responded, "It looked perfectly natural to me." A close-up of the scene was taken in which Shirley again shaded her eyes. Dozens of people have remarked to me about that particular scene.

In the same manner, Ford turned adverse conditions and elements into an opportunity to develop impressive and dramatic scenes. We left the studio one morning with the sun shining brightly, but by the time we arrived on location in Chatsworth, California, where the British army outpost was built, a strong wind had come up that was whipping the tall eucalyptus trees that surrounded the parade grounds back and forth. Dark storm clouds had begun gathering in the sky. We unloaded the camera equipment and placed it in one of the houses that faced the grounds. No one expected to do any work until the weather cleared, and that looked as though it might take a long time. Mr. Ford and I stood on the porch of the building, each holding a cup of coffee. As we watched the fast-moving dark clouds and the swaying trees, Ford turned to me and asked if I didn't think this would be a good time to do the burial sequence. After a moment's thought, I said I couldn't remember any burial sequence in the script. With a mischievous grin, he asked me the color of the cover of the revised script I had read. I told him it was blue. "That wasn't the final script," Ford said. By now I knew he had something in mind. To take advantage of the wind and elements, Ford had improvised a burial sequence of one of the officers and it blended smoothly into the story. A casket draped with a British Union Jack, resting on the flat bed of an army vehicle, drawn by four black horses and with an honor guard marching in slow step, and the wind whipping back and forth as though in protest against the menacing black clouds in the sky was one of the most dramatic and effective sequences in the picture.

Some say Ford tricked his actors to get them in the mood to play a particular scene. Maybe so, but he got the scene. As I said before, even after photographing several John Ford pictures, I didn't notice any pattern or method that could be used as a standard for comparison. He not only made each picture separate and different but each day of each picture was an individual and pleasurable experience.

Chapter 16

LAST FILMS BEFORE RETIREMENT

I N 1935 Darryl Zanuck took over the Fox studio and it became Twentieth Century-Fox Film Corporation. It was my good fortune to be chosen to photograph several of the pictures produced by Zanuck himself. All of them afforded me wonderful photographic opportunities. He was a perfectionist and would not accept anything that did not completely satisfy him. Once more I found myself in the delightful position of being able to exercise my own judgment as far as photography was concerned. This is not to say that at times Zanuck would not have a scene retaken, having suggested minor changes in the photography, but sometimes when it was obvious that the action of the scene had been drastically altered, I figured this was all part of the game. Mr. Zanuck's job was a difficult and complex one, for apart from producing his own pictures, he also managed the studio and had to handle the variety of temperaments that make up the motion picture business. He ran the film shot by every company working at Twentieth Century and supervised the editing of the final cut. There were, however, a couple of exceptions where the director controlled the editing. One of these was John Ford. Of the pictures personally produced by Zanuck, the ones that gave me the most satisfaction were *The Rains Came, The Razor's Edge, Anna and the King of Siam, The Ox-Bow Incident,* and, of course, *How Green Was My Valley.*

I had just returned from up north where we had been making some extra scenes along the Sacramento River for a picture called *Young Mr. Lincoln,* directed by John Ford, when Mr. Zanuck called me to his office to tell me that Clarence Brown, who had been borrowed from M.G.M. to direct *The Rains Came,* was dissatisfied and wanted to change the cameraman. They had just started the picture and had been shooting for only three days. If there is anything one cameraman hates to do it is to replace another, for often the replacement is due to a clash of personalities rather than the cameraman's work. Also it leaves a question as to what brought the change about and the possibility that the problem may still exist.

My orders were to take over the photographing of the picture at noon the next day. The stars of the picture were Myrna Loy and George Brent. This was the first time I had met Clarence Brown, who well understood my awkward position. During our conversation, he asked if I wanted to spend the afternoon taking some tests of Miss Loy that we could look at the next morning. He seemed a bit surprised when I told him I had photographed Miss Loy before and thought it would be all right to continue shooting the picture. We walked over to Miss Loy together and Brown went through the formalities of an introduction. Then he said, "Arthur tells me that he has photographed you before." With an expression of wonderment she asked, "When?" I answered, "In a picture at Warner Brothers, starring Loretta Young, that Bill Seiter directed." She thought a moment, and I continued, "You played the vamp in the picture." "Oh, that was a long time ago," Miss Loy responded, taking the whole thing in good humor. The picture was *The Truth About Youth,* made in 1930. It was now 1940, ten years later, during which time Miss Loy had become a star.

Predictably, our first shot was a close-up of Miss Loy. Among the lighting equipment was a small light called a match box, about eight inches square. All it was ever used for, when placed in the proper position, was to reflect light in the eyes of the person being photographed, thus producing a sparkle. We were just ready to shoot the close-up when Brown asked me if I would put a red gelatin in front of the match box light. I surmised that this was Miss Loy's wish, but she thought it would be more diplomatic if the director made the request. The tin box attached to the stand of the match box contained a couple of the red gelatins and so I obligingly placed one in front of the light. I thought it was a small enough gesture to make someone happy. We took the shot and Brown asked for another take. This time he asked if I would remove the red gelatin, which I did, and we proceeded to make the second take. We did a fair amount of work that afternoon, considering the situation.

The next morning in the projection room besides me there were Clarence Brown, Myrna Loy, and George Brent. I had completely forgotten the incident of the red gelatin, but I was anxious to see how well her close-ups came out, as people do change a little in ten years. The first take of the close-up of Miss Loy came on the screen, then the second take. Brown pressed the button, signaling the operator to stop running the film. The lights came on in the room and Brown started his speech. "I'm going to have the film of the close-up we just looked at run again, to show there is no difference in the quality of the eyes with the red gelatin on the light or without it." The room was darkened and the film run again. Brown proved his point, for there was no difference with or without the red gelatin. Some cameraman must have tried to gild the lily by using a red gelatin to make a hit with some star. In those days one star couldn't have something without every other one wanting it too. In reality, the red gelatin on the match box or eye light, as we used to call it, lost its effectiveness in photographing blue eyes because of the brightness of the key and filler lights necessary. I continued using the match box to produce a catch light in the eyes when shooting close-ups but dispensed with the red gelatin from that day on.

For *The Rains Came*, the entire floor of one stage was covered with tin to form a large pan to protect the floor. All the interiors and exterior sets that required rain, as well as the background shots, were photographed on this stage, which meant about ninety percent of the picture. For every set-up rain spouts were properly placed to simulate the sort of daily downpour that always occurs during the monsoon season in India.

After working on the stage all day in the rain, it was a surprise that it wasn't raining outside. Films of this type, where the effect really played a part in the picture, presented a considerable challenge that most cinematographers enjoyed, especially when the results were gratifying. *The Rains Came* was released in a sepia tone. In this instance, it helped to enhance the photography.

Edmund Goulding directed *The Razor's Edge*. He used a system of photographing each complete sequence from beginning to end with the camera shooting from a crane following the actors. This was supposed to achieve a continuous, smooth, fluid action. We rehearsed all morning and made the take before lunch, then rehearsed another sequence during the afternoon and shot it all before leaving the studio in the evening. The actors were required to memorize the dialogue for the entire sequence and had to make all their moves and pauses for dialogue precisely to the marks made during the rehearsals, so that the movement of the crane and the action would coincide. Zanuck looked at the rushes for about three days before deciding that both the action and dialogue appeared mechanical. He then called a halt to this method of shooting. Zanuck wanted medium shots and plenty of close-ups to play with when the time came to edit a picture.

Just before starting *Anna and the King of Siam,* a strike was called by the Carpenters Union. William Darling, one of the best directors in the business, came up with the idea of casting the sets in plaster. He had about ten units cast so they could be arranged to form sets of different angles. Casters were fastened to the bottom of each section to facilitate moving it about. All the fancy patterned scroll designs that filled the windows were cast in the mould along with its particular section. The white plaster had a matte surface and this eliminated the problem of reflections. No paint or stain whatsoever was applied. After a few tests, it was obvious that the problem was solved, and that this substitution presented an opportunity for a picture of high photographic quality.

Little did I know that a much more serious problem was in the making for me. When photographing a feminine star for the first time, it was customary to make a test or two to figure out her best photographic angles. The female star of the picture was Miss Irene Dunne to whom I was introduced the morning we were to shoot the test. Close-ups are equally important to the cinematographer and to the actress. A close-up is nothing more or less than a portrait—with the important difference that the subject moves, exposing various angles of the face. To photograph Miss Dunne, I placed a key or highlight source coming from a three-quarter angle from above and a filler light for the shadows about eye level from the front. Miss Dunne sat on a stool that revolved. As we rolled the camera I asked her to look in different directions to show the front side, three-quarter angle, and general contour of her face. This was a habit left over from the days when I had dabbled in portraiture. When I looked at the film, it told me what angles to avoid and what features I should try to emphasize. This test, of course, was for my own education, but somehow the editor showed it to Miss Dunne. I can just imagine what she thought when she saw it. The result was that I was called on the carpet in Mr. Zanuck's office. He wanted to know what had happened to me and said he could do better himself. At the end of my explanation that Miss Dunne was not supposed ever to have seen the test, Zanuck told me in terms not to be repeated here to have the production office set a date for me to make a test that she could see.

On the test stage the second time, I tried to make Miss Dunne feel a little more secure by asking her which cameraman she thought had photographed her best in all the pictures she had made and promised to call him and get all the information I could to enable me to photograph her in the same way. She gave me three names; all were good friends of mine. We decided to postpone the test until I talked to the other cinematographers. I actually did call the three she had mentioned and all cooperated willingly. At our next meeting on the test stage, I told Miss Dunne I had talked to all three men, but I could see that this news did not fill her with confidence. I realized there were some unpleasant days ahead.

When we started *Anna and the King of Siam*, Miss Dunne,

as I suspected, was worried and not too friendly. After about a week, the first vocal objection came. We were shooting a close-up and after I had set the lights and said I was ready, Miss Dunne said in utter despair, not to me but for my benefit, that she couldn't understand how a close-up of her could be lighted in a few minutes when other cameramen took at least half an hour. Up to this time she had refused to look at any of the film we had shot on the picture. As we finished the second week, the telephone near the entrance of the set rang. It was the editor telling the assistant director that the rushes were ready to be seen in one of the projection rooms. Miss Dunne heard the assistant director repeat this to the director, John Cromwell. Cromwell asked if she would like to look at the rushes. During the two weeks of shooting, apparently Miss Dunne's anxiety had built up to the breaking point, and Cromwell's suggestion had the effect of pulling the cork out of a champagne bottle. She turned to me and told me what misery she had gone through for the past two weeks; that she hadn't had a good night's sleep since we started the picture for worry about how she was being photographed and, to top it off, she said that she had learned that I didn't want to photograph the picture in the first place.

After Miss Dunne got it all out of her system, she defiantly accompanied Cromwell to the projection room. When she saw the rushes she was surprised and told me so. From then on she was one of the most cooperative actresses I have ever photographed, and I found that she knew all the tricks of the trade. In time I realized that it was not the usual vanity that was bothering her but my rather direct approach to lighting her. She assumed that I was disinterested, that it was just another picture to me, and that I wanted to get it over fast. She was a self-disciplined professional actress who took her work seriously and simply couldn't understand anyone she thought didn't feel the same way. Everything turned out well at the end, and I was gratified to hear that when she went to Warner Brothers studio for her next picture, Miss Dunne tried to borrow me from Twentieth Century to photograph her.

The Ox-Bow Incident, directed by William Wellman, told a

story of mob psychology. A posse of hot-headed cowboys hanged three men for cattle-rustling, only to find out later that the men were innocent. The posse rode into the mountain camp of their victims in the early evening, held a kangaroo court through the night, found them guilty and decided to wait until daybreak to hang them. Our mountain camp was built on a stage surrounded by a sky backing. A large oak tree was placed to form the central point of interest, with a small stream that helped the composition. About eight feet in front of the backing, painted cutouts were used for the distant horizon. Moonlight and a fire made by the men to keep themselves warm were supposed to provide the source of light until daybreak began to glow on the distant horizon. This was accomplished by lighting the backing from the floor. As the overall light was increased on the general scene, the sky backing was lighted from above, creating the effect of dawn. At this point, lighting became a part of the dramatic story being unfolded. The unfortunate men were placed on horses and led under a large branch grotesquely extending from the trunk of the tree. There three ropes hung and nooses were thrown around the necks of the victims. Just as a ray of sunshine broke through producing the effect of morning, the horses were whipped from under the men and the cowboys rode off, leaving the bodies suspended at the end of the ropes. The photography in *Ox-Bow Incident* was highly praised, as it would be in any picture where the photography becomes as important as a character in the script and actually plays a part in enhancing the dramatic value of the picture.

How Green Was My Valley was made in the usual John Ford manner — no problems. The Welsh village was built on the Twentieth Century ranch in San Fernando Valley, about an hour's ride from the studio. As a large part of the picture was played in the village, it became a daily routine for me to stop at the studio on my way to the location each morning to look at the rushes (the film photographed the day before) with the editor. It may surprise people to know that John Ford never looked at the daily rushes. The first film he saw on the screen was after the picture was completely photographed. I

How Green Was My Valley. Shooting a scene on the slag heap, at Twentieth Century ranch near Malibu Lake.

imagine the reason for this is that he seldom makes a second take of a scene; therefore there was no selection of takes to be made. Ford saw the scene when it was photographed and had no reason to see it again on the screen the next day. I might also mention that none of the actors saw any film until the picture had been edited and was ready to be shown to an audience. In picture-making, sometimes an actor, after he has seen the day's work on the screen, will try to improve his performance and in doing so change his characterization, which can mix things up a bit. Ford concentrated on the entire picture at all times — never on a single day's work. There was not a dolly or a boom shot in the entire picture. Occasionally, for the sake of composition or to accommodate the action, the camera would make a slight pan or tilt, but the mechanics of a roving camera never became noticeable.

A good illustration of the technique used in *How Green Was My Valley* is the shot of Maureen O'Hara leaving the church

John Ford with dark glasses taking his cue to call "action" in *How Green Was My Valley* as the assistant cameraman drops the number block from in front of the lens on the Twentieth Century-Fox silent camera. At left, Roddy MacDowall stands ready as Miller at extreme right watches intently.

after being married. The bride and groom came down the stone steps from the church, built on a small rise, and they moved through the gathering of well-wishers and got into a waiting carriage. The carriage, drawn by two horses, promptly pulled out of the scene. The camera panned slightly to the left in a hardly noticeable manner to show the minister who had performed the wedding ceremony and who had consequently lost forever the girl he loved. The minister was standing near the entrance to the church framed by a large oak tree, just a tiny figure in the distance. This was one of those rare occasions when Ford did his thinking out loud. Looking at the minister in the distance for a few seconds, he mumbled, "If I make a close-up, somebody will want to use it." Dismissing the thought, we moved to another location in the village and started shooting another sequence.

For many directors this would have been the perfect scene to shoot from a boom. As the carriage pulled out, they would have had the camera swing on in to a close-up of the minister to get the reaction on his face and thought that they had come up with a great piece of camera movement, forgetting that they would have lost the dramatic impact of that tiny figure which allowed the audience to imagine his thoughts and anguish for themselves.

After I saw the rushes at the studio each morning, I proceeded on to the location. Ford looked at the light tests (a strip of film about one foot long showing the scene at different printing lights). The light tests were all he saw of the film we shot during the photographing of the picture.

While we were shooting at the village location, Howard Jones, U.S.C. football coach and a friend of Ford's, visited the set. He, Ford, and I took our box lunches up to the top of the hill to rest and eat under a large, shady tree. After Ford had questioned Jones about his football team in general, Jones asked Ford if he thought he had a good picture in the making. Ford replied, "Everything seems fine but the picture tells a sad story of a family whose happy life has been practically destroyed by dire circumstances. The father has been killed in a mine disaster as well as one of the sons who left his new bride a widow. The daughter foolishly marries a man she doesn't love, and three grown sons leave to seek their fortunes in America. I have to find some way to bring the family together as far as the audience is concerned for them really to enjoy the picture." A few days later the blue sky was filled with huge, beautiful, white billowy clouds. After looking at the magnificent sight for a short time, Ford asked me if it would be possible to make those clouds appear larger on a process screen if we played the actors in front of them. We photographed a few cloud formations and projected them on the large, fifty-foot process screen. The art director built several compositions in front of the screen. One was a sloping hillside with a lone tree, and there were others. Ford played scenes in front of these, and in this manner he reviewed the cast. This had the effect he thought it would. When the picture was shown, some members of the cast drew applause during the review, and the audience left the theater in a happy frame of mind.

William Perlberg produced *The Song of Bernadette* and Henry King directed it. The village of Lourdes was built on the back lot at the studio and was an extensive construction job. Great attention was paid to detail of the period. The grotto where Bernadette saw her vision was a massive plaster job with rock ledges and other details. A huge constructed, painted background blocked the main thoroughfare that ran past the studio on Pico Boulevard. When construction of this magnitude is underway in preparation for the making of a picture, one realizes the responsibility that someone at the top must carry. It is not often that a director has the opportunity of starting work on the first sequence of a picture. Where he starts usually depends on economics, such as stage space for the sets, whether certain actors are available, and if it is to be shot outside, the weather prospects, particularly if the location is a distant one. *Bernadette* was one picture that we were able to begin with the first sequence, the interior of Bernadette's home. Henry King, with his years of experience, played three or four sequences. Then he made the exteriors that were to be sandwiched in, giving him about three completed reels of the beginning of the picture. Weeks later, after we finished the day's work, his editor had the three reels run in the projection room. Nobody predicted that it would be a successful picture although it was already obvious. The entire film was made in the studio and on the back lot, with the exception of a few scenes that were made at Cherry Valley near Beaumont, California.

The second picture I photographed for Henry King was a far cry from the spiritual background of *The Song of Bernadette*. It was *Gun Fighter*, produced by Nunnally Johnson and starring Gregory Peck. In this picture men depended upon their six-shooters for survival. The western street was on the back lot. Originally built in the late twenties, it was now over half

a mile long, with little side streets and alleys branching off the
main street. We used the same western street for *Ox-Bow
Incident*.

Henry King liked to shoot without the use of background
process whenever possible, so many of the interiors were shot
in the buildings on the street. Under these circumstances,
whenever a shot looks through a window or door, the age-old
problem of balancing the exposure of the interior with the
daylight of the exterior arises. This sometimes compels the
cinematographer to build the light on the interior to the point
where the actors are uncomfortable with the brightness of
the lights and some of them fuss. Although *Gun Fighter* was a
western picture, its outstanding success was due to the director
and fine performances of the actors.

Darryl Zanuck was now spending most of his time in Europe
producing pictures there. Many changes had taken place at
Twentieth Century-Fox, and the final option of my contract
was coming to an end. I now had lost contact with the head
man and was forced to deal with the head of the production
department who, in my opinion, lacked appreciation for art or
quality. His main object seemed to be the cutting of costs. Consequently I ran into trouble over the terms of a new contract.
After about two weeks of quibbling over terms and eighteen
years of photographing pictures for the company, I left and
signed a contract with Sam Spiegel and John Huston, co-
partners in Horizon Pictures. I was anxious to work with
director John Huston but unfortunately he was preparing for
his next picture. Joe Losey directed the first one for the partnership and it was called *The Prowler*. After finishing this film,
I was laid low with tuberculosis and never had the opportunity
of making such pictures as *African Queen, Bridge on the River
Kwai,* or *Lawrence of Arabia,* all produced by Sam Spiegel.
Although I have recovered from T.B., my general state of
health still will not permit me to return to active work.

Since that time one occasion of joy connected with the industry has come my way, and that was the night when John
Ford made the presentation of the Billy Bitzer Award to me
on behalf of the International Photographers Alliance at one

Arthur C. Miller, protegé of Fred J. Balshofer, shown with the three Oscars he won for photographing *How Green Was My Valley, The Song of Bernadette,* and *Anna and the King of Siam.*

of their meetings. Since then I have devoted much of my time to the activities of the American Society of Cinematographers, and have served as its president for two terms. During these years I have started what has turned into a small museum, a collection of early moving picture cameras and projectors for the A.S.C. This collection is still growing. I remain a member of the Board of Cinematographers Union and have recently been elected to the Board of Governors of the Academy of Motion Picture Arts and Sciences.

Now that Fred Balshofer and I are both in retirement, we have had the time to scratch out these first-hand records of our past joint motion picture careers. Although Fred is eighty-nine, his memory and alertness are truly remarkable. Going back over the past has brought to mind many incidents that seemed grave to us then but the passage of time has converted them into trivial and even humorous matters.

A goodly portion of the early history of motion pictures
seems to have been based on the stories of press agents. Then
as now, press agents wrote releases only for the purpose of
building an image of importance for some personality active
in the industry. Since this element served no purpose for our
account, we hope that the elimination of it has left only a record
of a little segment of the true history of the beginning and
growth of movie-making in the United States.

Fred J. Balshofer, 87, is awarded an honorary membership in the American Society of Cinematographers in 1965 by president Ray Rennahan
for his many contributions to the motion picture industry.

Pictorial Appendix

The following illustrations provide relatively recent examples of the cameraman's art, for contrast with the earlier shots included in the text. They are enlargements of test shots (made in the movie camera) from films photographed by Arthur C. Miller.

Brigham Young

Mark of Zorro

Tobacco Road

How Green Was My Valley

How Green Was My Valley

How Green Was My Valley

The Ox-Bow Incident

Keys to the Kingdom

The Song of Bernadette

Anna and the King of Siam

A Letter to Three Wives

Index

Film titles are given in *italics*. Names of magazines are given in CAPITAL LETTERS.

Aaronson. *See* Anderson, Broncho Billy
Academy of Motion Picture Arts and Sciences, 201
Acord, Art, 58, 64, 66, 75
Actaphone, 48
Adams, Cora, 106, 123
African Queen, 200
Aitkin, Harry, 92
Alder, William, 117, 119
Allen, Eugene, 64
Aller, Joe, 119
Allison, May, 136–138
American Federation of Labor, 178
American Flying "A" Studios, 136
AMERICAN MAGAZINE, 132
American Mutoscope & Biograph Company, 2, 6, 10, 12, 24
American Society of Cinematographers, 146, 201, 202
Anderson, Broncho Billy, 55, 79, 113, 141
Anderson, Captain, 32
Anderson, Gilbert M., *See* Anderson, Broncho Billy
Angel of Broadway, The, 49
Anna and the King of Siam, 189, 192, 193, 205
Aranson, William, 115
Arbuckle, Roscoe "Fatty," 81, 138
Arms and the Woman, 129, 132
Arnold, Edward, 180
Arnold, John, 52
Asher, Efe, 117, 119, 120
Astra Film Company, 124, 132, 133, 143, 145
At Bay, 124–127
At Coney Island, 77
Avalanche, The, 148
Avar, 73
Avenue Theater, 106
Avery, Charles, 55, 58
Ayres, Lew, 180

Bachrach, Ernest, 156
Bacon, Frank, 121
Bacon, Lloyd, 121
Ball, J. A., 167, 168
Balshofer, Fred J., 1–30, 32–37, 38–42, 43, 44, 46, 48–51, 53, 55–67, 73, 74–93, 108–123, 136–142, 201, 202

Baron Long's Country Club, 86, 111, 112
Barrymore, John, 153, 154
Barrymore, Lionel, 154
Barthelmess, Richard, 143, 154, 155
Barton, Steve, 64
Bauman, Charles O., 16, 22, 24–28, 38, 59, 60, 62, 67, 75–77, 83, 84, 88, 90–93, 108–110
Bayne, Beverly, 115, 120, 121
"Behind the Screen," 118
Bell & Howell, 66, 78-79, 82, 143, 152, 164, 185, 186
Bell, Donald, 78, 79, 82, 89, 90
Bell, Monta, 172
Bella Donna, 164
Bellamy Trial, The, 171
Bennett, Constance, 167
Bennett, Joan, 181
Bennett, Spencer, 97
Bennett, Whitman, 152
Bergere, Ouida (Mrs. George Fitzmaurice), 124, 149–152, 154, 156, 162, 165
Bianchi camera, 52, 98
Bickford, Charles, 179
Big Bear Valley, 63–66, 74, 121
Big Jim Garrity, 126
Billy Bitzer Award, 200
Biograph, 7, 12, 26, 28, 34, 41, 49, 55, 67, 77, 109, 167
Birth of A Nation, 34
Bison Company, 25, 28, 29, 39, 40, 48, 50, 55, 57–59, 63, 65, 66, 74, 76, 77, 79, 80, 89, 91, 138, 141, 142
Bitzer, William (Billy), 34, 49, 55, 71, 150
Bloom, Jack, 145, 146
Blondeau's Tavern, 111
Blood and Sand, 139
Boggs, Francis, 55, 57
Bosworth, Hobart, 57
Bowman, William, 121
Boyd, Bill, 169, 171
Boyle Heights, 74, 84
Brandenburg's Dime Museum, 6
Brandt, Joe, 140
Brenon, Herbert, 67
Brent, George, 190, 191
Bridge on the River Kwai, 200

211

Brigham Young, 205
Bright Eyes, 181
Broadway Bill, 137
Broken Blossoms, 34, 150
Broncho Films, 91
Bronson, Betty, 172
Brooks, Jim, 76, 80, 85
Brown, Clarence, 190, 191
Brown, John Mack, 173
Brown, Milt, 55
Brownie camera, 18
Brulatour, Jules, 25, 38
Brunner, 166, 167
Brunton studio, 146, 167, 177
Buckley, 135
Burston, Louis, 24
Burt, William, 135
Bushman, Francis X., 114–121
Butler, David, 181

C.B.C. Pictures, 140
Caluci, Arturo, 166
Cameraphone, 48
Cantor, Eddie, 3
Card, James, 118
Carleton, William, 149
Carpentier, Georges, 157, 160
Castle, Irene, 132, 133
Castle, Vernon, 133
Cella, Pete, 27
Centaur, 21, 50
Chadwick, Cyril, 161, 162
Chadwick, Helene, 135
Champion Company, 84
Chaplin, Charles, 81, 90, 91, 108, 113, 114
Chaplin, Sydney, 113
Chatterton, Ruth, 171
Chauncey Proves A Good Detective, 19
Cheat, The, 146, 164
Christie, Al, 121
Christie, Charles, 121, 137
Christie Film Company, 121
Church, Fred, 141
Cinema Camera Club, 123, 146
Cinematographer's Union, 201
Clark, Whitey, 111
Clark's Halfway House, 64
Clawson, Dal, 145, 146
Clifford, William, 117, 121, 138, 139
Clock, The, 62
Cody, Lew, 145
Cohen At Coney Island, 77
Cohn, Harry, 140, 141
Cohn, Jack, 140, 141

Colman, Ronald, 168
Coliseum Film Producing Company, 158, 160
Columbia Broadcasting, 121
Columbia Phonograph Company, 98
Columbia Pictures Corporation, 140, 141
Common Clay, 145
Compson, Betty, 147
Conklin, Chester, 81
Conklin, Heinie, 81
Conway, Jack, 58, 64, 75
Cooney, 96, 100
Cooper-Hewitt lighting, 6, 43, 45, 47, 94, 95, 122, 125, 129, 133, 143, 146
Cooper, Tex, 55, 58
Corner In Cotton, A, 121
Counterfeit, The, 149
Coytesville. *See* Fort Lee
Crammer, Gus, 152
Crane, Frank, 133
Crescent Film Company, 15, 17, 21, 22, 37, 52, 77
Cromwell, John, 194
Crystal studio, 52, 53
Cummings, Irving, 98
Cuneo, Lester, 117, 119, 121, 138
Curley, Pauline, 138
Cytherea, 167

Daniels, Bebe, 58, 75
Daniels, Phyllis, 58, 75
Darkfeather, Princess Mona, 58, 64
Darling, William, 192
Darrel, Jewell, 55, 58
Daugherty, Harry, 157
Davies, Howard, 58
Davy Crockett In Hearts United, 27
Defender Film Company, 45, 47, 50
DeMille, Cecil B., 49, 164, 168, 169, 170, 171, 173–175, 177ff.
Dempsey-Brennon fight, 159
Dempsey, Jack, 157, 160
Desperate Character, A, 21
Dexter, Eliot, 154
Diamond Jim, 180
Dillon, Edward, 40, 41
Dillon, Jack, 148
Dintenfass, Mark, 48, 84
Disinherited Son's Loyalty, 26
Dobbs, George, 85
Dobson, George, 11, 12
Dr. Jekyll and Mr. Hyde, 153, 154
Doll House Baby, 123
Domino, 91

Doraldena, 133
Dressler, Marie, 81, 91
Drew, John, 117, 121
Dunne, Irene, 193f.
Durfee, Minta (Mrs. Roscoe Arbuckle), 81

Eastman Kodak, 24, 25, 70, 171
Eclair, 84, 105, 109
Edendale, 66, 74, 76, 81, 82, 85–89
Edison, 2, 6, 7, 9, 10, 12, 13, 17, 18, 24, 38, 39, 47, 50, 52, 62, 98, 171
Edmonds, Buster, 62, 63
Edwards, Bill, 40, 54
Edwards, Gus, 3
Eltinge, Julian, 139
Elvey, Maurice, 162
Empire Film Exchange, 16, 22
Engadine Amusement Company, 52
Engel, Joseph, 45, 46, 48, 50–52, 84, 114, 136, 137
Erwin, Stu, 181
Esmeralda Inn, 137
Esperanto Film Company, 106, 107, 114, 116, 122, 123
Essanay, 12, 24, 55, 79, 113–115, 120, 123, 124
Eternal City, The, 51, 165, 166
Experience, 154, 155

Fair, Elinor, 169
Famous Players–Lasky Company, 53, 146, 147, 151, 152, 156, 163
Farnum, William, 57
Favar, Marguerite, 55, 58
Fawcett, George, 154, 156
Fazenda, Louise, 81, 110, 172
Feeding the Pigeons in Central Park, 2
Ferguson, Elsie, 51, 143ff.
Fifth Avenue, 126
Fireman's Parade on Fifth Avenue, The, 2
Fisher, Paul, 106, 107
Fisherman's Romance, A, 26, 27
Fitzmaurice, George, 122–135, 146–150, 152, 155, 156, 164, 166, 168, 180
Florence, Giuseppe, 123
Ford, Francis, 138
Ford, Hugh, 51, 148, 150, 151
Ford, John, 156, 177-188, 189, 190, 195–200
Forever, 154, 156
Fort Lee, New Jersey, 27–39, 47, 48, 50, 97, 101, 105, 109, 159

Four Horsemen of the Apocalypse, The, 119, 139
Fox, 180, 189. See also Twentieth Century–Fox
Fox camera, 185, 197
Franconie, Leo, 68, 69, 72, 73
Franklyn, Chester, 110
Frawley, Jack, 6, 8, 9
Frederick, Pauline, 51
French, Charles, 26, 27, 28, 39, 40, 54, 55, 61
Frohman, Daniel, 52f.

Garland, Judy, 181
Garnett, Tay, 179, 180
Gasnier, Louis, 73, 96, 102, 104, 106, 124, 132, 134
Gaudio, Tony, 138
Gaumont, 6, 52, 68
Gebhardt, George, 58, 60, 61, 64, 66
Gebhardt, Madeline, 61
General Electric Company, 116, 122
Gentlemen Prefer Blondes, 121
George Eastman House, 118
Gibbons, William, 55
Gibson, Hoot, 64
Gill, Jack, 35
Goddard, Charles, 95
Goldwyn, Samuel, 164, 165, 167, 168
Gone With the Wind, 134
Gordon, Edward, 158
Goudal, Jetta, 169
Goulding, Edmund, 161, 192
Grable, Betty, 181
Graff–Verable lens, 150
Graham, Evelyn, 26–28, 33, 36, 39, 40, 54, 55, 75
Graham, Frank, 62, 63, 86, 89, 113
Grandon, Ethel, 76
Great Train Robbery, The, 2
Griffith, Beverly, 110
Griffith, David Wark, 49, 55, 93, 133, 150
Grot, Anton, 130–134, 147
Gun Fighter, The, 199, 200

Haas, Robert, 147
Hackett, Norman, 106, 122
Haley, Jack, 181
Hall Room Boys, The, 140
Hands Up, 134
Hansford Brown Company, 48
Hardy, Harry, 135
Harmon, Denver, 144
Hartigan, Pat, 75

Haunted Pajamas, 137, 138
Haver, Phyllis, 81
Hayakawa, Sessue, 145, 146, 164, 167
Headless Horseman, The, 171
Heck, Fred, 138
Hendricks restaurant, 131, 134, 147
Herbert, Holmes, 151
Heroine of '76, A, 48, 49
Hidden Springs, The, 137
High Road, The, 171
His First Command, 179
His House In Order, 150
His Supreme Moment, 168
Hitchcock, Alfred, 161
Hopper, E. Mason, 124
Horizon Pictures, 200
Horne, James, 134
Horsley, David, 21, 57, 75, 84, 85, 92, 110, 111, 119, 121
House of Hate, The, 134, 135
Houseman step-printer, 44
How Green Was My Valley, 156, 189, 195–197, 205
Howell, Albert S., 78
Hunsaker and Hunsaker, 89
Hurd, Earl, 157
Huston, John, 200

Idols of Clay, 154
Ihnen, Wiard (Bill), 147, 149, 150–152
Imp, 49, 50, 52, 67, 74, 83, 84, 140
Ince, Thomas H., 75, 76, 93, 169
Informer, The, 183
Inslee, Charles, 28, 29, 32–34, 36, 40, 54, 59, 64–67
International Photographer's Alliance, 200
Iron Heart, The, 132
Isle of Love, The, 139

Jacobs, Billy, 110
Jazz Singer, The, 172
Jeffries, Jim, 82, 121
Jeske, George, 81, 110, 112, 113
Jessel, George, 3, 172
Johnnie Out of the Ink Well, 157
Johnson, Justine, 148
Johnson, Nunnally, 199
Johnson, Olive, 110
Jolson, Al, 172
Jones, Howard, 198
Jones, Julia, 141
Jones, Tom, 86
Jourjon, Charles, 84
Joy, Leatrice, 49, 171, 172

Kalem, 12, 24
Kaybee, 91
Kellerman, Annette, 81
Kelly, Jack, 85
Kelly, Patsy, 181
Kennedy, Joseph P., 179
Kenny, May, 24, 92
Kerry, Norman, 161, 162
Kessel, Adam, 16, 22, 24, 26–28, 38, 59, 60, 62, 67, 77, 84, 85, 88, 91–93, 108–110
Kessel, Charles, 24, 25, 90
Keys to the Kingdom, 205
Keystone Film Company, 50, 74–93, 109, 111
Kinetoscope, 2
King, Henry, 156, 199, 200
Kipper, Charles, 35, 85
Kirkwood, James, 163
Klaw and Erlanger, 167
Kleigl Light Company, 122
Kleine, George, 12, 24, 52
Kolle, Herman, 14, 16–19, 21, 22
Kolle, William, 21
Kosloff, Theodore, 169

Ladies World Magazine, 115
Lady Rose's Daughter, 151f.
Laemmle, Carl, 52, 83–85, 88, 90, 92, 108, 114, 140
Lamphier, 35
Lane, George, 30, 35
Langdon, Harry, 179
LaRocque, Rod, 171
LaRue, Carmen, 110
Latham loop, 38
Law, Rodman, 100
Law, Ruth, 100
Lawrence of Arabia, 200
Lehr, Abe, 168
Lehrman, Henry "Pathé," 77, 80, 81, 91, 109–113
Lend Me Your Name, 137
Leonard, Robert, 57, 154
Letter To Three Wives, 205
Lightnin', 121
Lion Tamer, The, 142
Little, Ann (Anna), 58, 64, 138
Little Dove's Gratitude, 65
Little Dove's Romance, 63
Little Miss Broadway, 98
Lockwood, Harold, 136–139
Loos, Anita, 121
Lopat, Rodriguez, 141
Losey, Joe, 200

Love, Montagu, 154
Loy, Myrna, 190, 191
Lubin Manufacturing Company, 1, 10–12, 14, 19, 24
Lubin, Siegmund, 4–9
Lumière, 6, 10, 25, 30, 38, 104
Lyman, Bill, 156, 157, 160
Lyman, Mike, 111
Lyon and Lyon, 62f.

M.G.M., 171, 172, 190
MacDowall, Roddy, 197
Mace, Fred, 77, 80, 86, 87, 91
Macgowan, Kenneth, 118, 119
MacKenzie, Donald, 96f.
Mahan, Jack, 86
Man From Home, The, 162, 166
Man of Honor, 137
Mann, Hank, 81
Mansfield, Martha, 138
Mark of Cain, The, 132
Mark of Zorro, 205
Martin, Tony, 181
Marx, Groucho, 3
McCarey, Leo, 86
McCarey, Tom, 86, 87
McDonald, 162
McGaugh, Jess, 55, 58, 59, 141
McCoy, Al "Slim," 17–19, 21, 34, 36–41, 47, 57, 60, 61, 66
McGuire, Major, 55
McLaglen, Victor, 184, 187
Me and My Gal, 181
Méliès, Georges, 5, 6, 8
Menzies, William Cameron, 132, 134, 181
Merry Widow, The, 170
Metro, 114, 136, 137
Meyers, Carmel, 138
Miles Brothers, 11, 12
Mill, Louis, 106, 123
Miller, Arthur C., 19, 22, 23, 25, 26, 29, 30–37, 40, 41, 42, 43–53, 54, 68–73, 94–107, 109, 114, 116, 122–135, 143–204
Miller, Mrs. Arthur C., 135, 166, 169
Miller Brothers 101 Ranch, 76, 78, 79
Miller, Charlie, 185
Miller, Joe, 76, 79, 80
Miller, Zack, 80
Millhauser, Bertram, 96, 102
Million Dollar Mystery, 117
Mitchell camera, 164–166, 172, 174, 183, 185, 186

Montgomery, Frank E., 55, 58, 64
Moore, Owen, 136
Moran, Lee, 140
Moran, Polly, 81
Moreno, Antonio, 132–135
Mosher and Harrington, 11, 12
Motion Picture Distributors and Sales Co., 47
Motion Picture Patents Company. See Patents Company
Mouquin's French Restaurant, 24
MOVING PICTURE WORLD, 41
Murphy, Frank, 144
Murphy, George, 98
Murray, Charles, 81, 91
Murray, Mae, 143–154
Mussolini, Benito, 163, 165, 166
Mutiny on the Bounty, 181
Mutoscope, 2

Nash, Mary, 129
Naulahka, The, 133, 134
Naulty, 152
Negri, Pola, 163, 164
Nestor Company, 21, 50, 84, 111, 121
Newhard, Robert, 48, 61, 67
New York, 126
New York Motion Picture Company, 15, 22, 23, 24, 30, 35, 50, 54, 68, 75, 76, 79, 82, 84, 89, 91–93, 108, 109
Nilsson, Anna Q., 161, 162, 168f.
Normand, Mabel, 77, 80, 81, 91, 108, 109
Nungesser's Roadhouse, 105

101 Bison brand pictures. See Bison
O.K. America, 180
Obrock, Herman, 15, 16, 19, 52, 53, 68, 69
O'Hara, Maureen, 196
On With the Dance, 149ff.
Ortega, Art, 58, 64, 141
Osborn, Baby Marie, 145
Osborne, Bud, 141
Overbaugh, Roy, 153f.
Ox-Bow Incident, The, 189, 194, 195, 200, 205

Paley, William, 52
Panama Flo, 179
Panama Pacific Fair, 119
Panzer, Paul, 97, 99
Paradise Garden, 137, 139
Paramount, 146, 168, 169

Patents Company, 24, 26, 34, 36, 38–42, 50, 60, 62–64, 74, 81, 83, 91, 92, 98
Pathé camera, 11f., 14f., 61, 70f., 97, 106f., 143, 152
Pathé Frères, 6, 24, 68ff., 94–107, 109, 114, 124, 125f.
Pathé News Weekly. *See Pathé Frères*
Paying the Piper, 154
Peacock Alley, 154
Pearce, Peggy, 81, 110
Peck, Gregory, 199
Pennington's Choice, 120
Perils of Pauline, The, 73, 94–107
Perlberg, William, 199
Peter Ibbetson, 154, 155
Peters, T. K., 55
Pickford, Mary, 55, 136
Pidgin Island, 137f.
Pier Thirteen, 181
Pigskin Parade, 181
Pitch, 96, 100
Porter, Edwin S., 2, 41, 43–53, 73, 94
Powell, David, 152
Powell, Frank, 105
Powers Film Company, 50, 83, 84, 97, 98
Powers, Pat, 83, 84, 88, 92, 98
Powers Picture Players. *See* Powers Film Company
Powers projector, 15
Prevost, Marie, 81
Profiteers, The, 145
Promise, The, 137
Prospect Hall, 14, 15, 17, 19, 21
Prowler, The, 200
Purden, Roy, 58, 64

Quality Pictures Corporation, 114–116, 119, 121
Queen Kelly, 179

R.C.A., 173
R.K.O., 179
Rain, 181
Rains Came, The, 189–192
Rambo's Saloon and Hotel, 31, 32, 34, 37, 97, 109
Rappe, Virginia, 138, 139
Rathbone, Basil, 171
Razor's Edge, The, 189, 192
Recoil, The, 132
Red Wing, 28, 33, 36, 40, 54, 55, 63, 75
Redman, Frank, Jr., 135

Redman, Frank, Sr., 96
Reed, Florence, 124, 125
Reichenbach, Harry, 115–117, 119, 120
Reid, Wallace, 136, 154–156
Reinhard, 35
Rennahan, Ray, 168, 202
Rex Film Company, 48, 50–52, 84, 94
Rich, Irene, 167
Richard, Al, 28, 35–38, 46, 68, 69, 73
Rickard, Tex, 157, 159
Right to Love, 152
Riley and Schultz, 77
Rivers, Joe, 86f.
Robertson, John, 148, 153
Rogers, Will, 171
Roland, Richard, 114, 136, 137
Roland, Ruth, 134
Romantic Journey, 132
Roosevelt, Theodore, 12
Rosemary, 121
Rosenberg, Aaron, 181
Rubens, Alma, 167
Rucker, Joe, 69, 70
Russia, Country of Depression, 46

Sadie Thompson, 181
St. Francis Hotel, 119
Sais, Marin, 58, 75
Santa Monica, 74, 80, 81, 85, 93
Santa Monica Water & Power Company, 74
Santschi, Tom, 57
Sartov, Henry, 150
Schable, Bob, 152
Schildkraut, Joe, 171
Schmidt, Hans, 15
Schneider, Eberhard, 25, 43, 78
Second In Command, The, 117–119, 121
Sedgwick, Edward, 138
See America Thirst, 179
Seibel, Bert, 85
Seiter, William, 179, 190
Seitz, George B., 96, 101, 102, 134, 135
Seitz, John, 119
Selby, Gertrude, 81
Selig, William N., 12, 24, 54, 56, 57
Selznick, 134
Sennett, Mack, 77, 80–83, 87–89, 91, 93, 109, 110
Sherer, George, 82f.
Sherry, J. Barney, 40, 54, 55, 64, 75
Shields Lantern Slide Company, 3, 4
Simplex, 51, 116
Sisson, Vera, 138, 139

Skate on Skates, A, 17
Smalley, Phillips, 49
Smallwood, Ray, 76, 87, 137
Smith, Maxwell, 41, 48, 54, 55, 61, 75
Snow, Marguerite, 117, 119, 121
Snowball, 59
Society Exile, 149
Solax, 133
Song of Bernadette, The, 156, 199, 205
Sperry, 143
Spiegel, Sam, 200
Spoor, George K., 55, 79, 113
Square Deceiver, The, 137
Squaw's Revenge, A, 28
Standing, Jack, 98
Stanlaws, Penrhyn, 132, 147
Static Club, 146
Steiner, William, 52, 84
Sterling Film Company, 108–114
Sterling, Ford, 77, 80, 91, 108–113
Stevens, Leo, 101, 102
Stone, Lewis, 167
Stromeyer and Wyman, 1
Summerville, Slim, 179
Sunset Boulevard, 119
Swanson, Gloria, 81, 179, 181
Swanson, William, 48, 50, 84–90, 92
Sweet, Blanche, 168
Sylvia of the Secret Service, 132, 133

Tarnish, 168
Technicolor Corporation, 167, 168
Temple, Mrs., 181, 182, 187
Temple, Shirley, 98, 181–184, 187, 188
Ten Commandments, The, 164
Thanhouser Company, 98
Thaw, Evelyn Nesbit, 9
Thaw, Harry K., 9
Thief In Paradise, A, 168
Thornby, Bob, 110, 112
Three Live Ghosts, 161, 162
Tillie's Punctured Romance, 91, 113
To Have and To Hold, 163
Tobacco Road, 205
Too Many Girls, 47
Toot, the Tailor, 124
Tracy, Spencer, 181
Triangle, 92, 93, 108
Trip to the Moon, A, 8
Troublesome Baby, 17
True Heart of An Indian, The, 28, 29, 30–38
Truth About Youth, The, 190
Tucker, George Loane, 67

Turner, 137
Turpin, Ben, 81
Twelvetrees, Helen, 179
Twentieth Century–Fox, 189, 194–197, 200

Under Handicap, 137
Underwood and Underwood, 1–4
Universal, 84–86, 88–92, 108, 109, 112, 143, 179, 180

Valentino, Rudolph, 139
Van Buren, Ned, 171
Varconi, Victor, 169
Veeder counter, 127
Vengeance Is Mine, 133
Verito lens, 150
Verno, 105
Via Wireless, 124
Villa Richard, 105
Vitagraph, 6, 12, 24, 81
Volga Boatman, The, 169, 171
Von Stroheim, Erich, 132, 145, 179

Waldron, Charles, 127
Walsh, Raoul, 180f.
Walters, Walter, 35
Walthall, Henry B., 55
Wanderer of the Wasteland, 168
Ward, Fanny, 134, 145, 146
Warner Brothers, 171, 174, 179, 180, 190, 194
Water Nymph, A, 81
Way Down East, 34
Wayside Inn, 153
Weber, Lois, 49
Wee Willie Winkie, 183
Wellman, William, 194
Wells, 157, 159
Welsbach gas mantle, 45
Westerburg, Billy, 85
Weston, Charlie, 76
What Not Company, 140
What Poverty Leads To, 19, 21
White, Pearl, 97, 99, 100–102, 104, 134, 135
White, Stanford, 9
Whiteman, Paul, 172
Whitman, 156–160
Wilbur, Crane, 97–100
Willat, C. A. (Doc), 67, 78, 85
Willat, Irwin, 168
Winchell, Walter, 3
Withey, Chet, 148
Witness for the Defense, The, 147, 148

Wolgast, Ad, 86f.
Wollensack lens, 150
Wood, A. H., 125
Wood, Harry, 73, 96
World, 50
World Film Company, 50
World–Peerless Studio, 109
Worsley, Ralph, 123
Worthington, William, 146
Wright, Walter, 87
Wurtzel, Sol, 181

Yacht Club Boys, 181
Yankee Film Company, 52, 84
Yorke Film Corporation, 136–142
Young Deer, 28, 33, 40, 54, 55, 63, 75
Young, Hal, 152
Young Heroes of the West, 17
Young, Loretta, 180, 190
Young Mr. Lincoln, 190

Zanuck, Darryl, 189, 190, 192, 193, 200
Zukor, Adolph, 52, 148